DIAG
F
LIV

DIAGRAMS FOR LIVING

The Bible Unveiled

EMMET FOX

HarperOne
An Imprint of HarperCollinsPublishers

HarperCollins books may be purchased for educational, business, or sales
promotional use. For information please e-mail the Special Markets Depart-
ment at SPsales@harpercollins.com.

HarperCollins Web site: http://www.harpercollins.com

HarperCollins®, ▦®, and HarperOne™ are trademarks of
HarperCollins Publishers.

FIRST HARPERCOLLINS PAPERBACK EDITION PUBLISHED IN 1993

Library of Congress Cataloging-in-Publication Data

Fox, Emmet.
    Diagrams for living : the Bible unveiled / Emmet Fox.
    p. cm.
Originally published: Harper & Row, 1968.
ISBN 978–0–06–250335–0
1. Bible—Criticism, interpretation, etc.   2. Conduct of life.
I. Title.
BS511.2.F68   1993   91–58895
220.6—dc20

HB 10.06.2022

Contents

Preface

T HE present volume fulfills another promise made by Emmet Fox to his students and friends to "unveil" a cross section of the Bible in narrative form; not only to make the Bible come alive for modern readers but also to open up to their consciousness the diagrams for living that the Bible has veiled in symbol and allegory.

To quote Dr. Fox: "Some people wonder why the Bible has to be unveiled at all, and the answer is that the Bible is written in symbol and allegory, for many reasons, but chiefly because that is the only method by which the teaching could be made fit for every kind of person at every stage of spiritual development in every age. While the Bible contains much authentic history and biography, it also contains a great mass of parables and allegories. The chief difficulty in modern times that intelligent people have had to meet is that they have not understood that some of the things in the Bible that used to be taught as fact are really allegory, and contain great diagrams of our personal destinies."

This book has been compiled from the hundreds of lectures and class lessons that Emmet Fox delivered to tens of thousands in such vast halls as Royal Albert Hall in London; Carnegie Hall in New York; the old Hippodrome and the Manhattan Opera House, where audiences numbered five to six thousand twice a week; the Biltmore and Astor hotels; the Palace Hotel in San Francisco; and many others in the United States and abroad.

H.W.

CHAPTER 1

Your Wrestling Angel

And Jacob was left alone; and there wrestled a man with him until the breaking of the day.

GENESIS 32:24

YOU are an important person with a glorious destiny and you have a wonderful biography written about you. It is a very different biography from the usual kind because in addition to being a personal history in which both achievements and shortcomings are noted, it shows you how to overcome difficulties and problems, and how to give expression to the deep aspirations that lie hidden in your soul. It outlines diagrams for living so that you can take the necessary steps to make your life worthwhile and interesting. This biography of you is called the Bible, and, whether you realize it or not, you are on every page from Genesis to Revelation.

The Bible is written in symbol and allegory. Some people know that; yet they continue to read the Bible in the literal way and consequently miss its message of spiritual

1

power. The veil is still over their hearts, as Paul remarked. What do I mean by "symbol"? According to Webster, a symbol is a "sign of . . . an idea." It is not the thing itself but it represents it, as the dove is a symbol of peace, and palms are a symbol of victory. In the parable of the Good Samaritan, a real man did not go down from Jerusalem on a particular day, nor did a certain Levite actually pass by. Jesus told the story to illustrate a point. In like manner, the story of Adam and Eve is an allegory to explain great spiritual Truths.

The reason why many people have given up the Bible is that they have taken it *literally*, whereas the Bible was meant to be taken spiritually. They say, "The story of Jonah and the whale cannot be true." Of course it is not true, in a literal sense. It is an allegory. Nor is it true that the Prodigal Son was a certain young man who went into a far country and then came back and was wined and dined by his father. These things are parables that come to life and reveal diagrams for living when we have the spiritual key.

Everything in the Bible is significant. All the characters, both male and female, illustrate and dramatize certain states of mind that could and do happen to people in this present day, in New York or Paris or Tokyo. The Bible is not just ancient history: it is a living thing for today.

You can find yourself in the Bible, but there is no guarantee you will be pleased when you do! However, if you do not like the picture you see, you can always change from one Bible character to another. In this great play the actors cast themselves. If they do not like the role they find themselves in, they can change to another because the Bible gives us the key to transforming life.

Just as every character in the Bible symbolizes a state of your soul, so does every incident in the Bible signify something that can happen to you. Abraham moving into Canaan; Jesus at the lakeside; Jesus going up to Jerusalem; Paul on the Road to Damascus—all these represent dramatic, powerful, colorful events in your life today, the things that either age you and give you heartbreak, or lift you up to new levels of joy and accomplishment. They are dramatic, symbolic diagrams for living to show *you* how you can come out of limitation and find real happiness.

Every name in the Bible has a meaning. For that matter, all names have a meaning. Your name represents the idea of you and your life. The life of every man and woman is a parable of the things that have happened to them since they were born. You were born in Los Angeles or Paris or Berlin, let us say. You went to certain schools and churches. You got such and such a job or entered this or that profession. You married or stayed single. You lived in a particular place and did certain things—good things or bad things, wise or foolish things. Your whole life is a parable that symbolizes the kind of person you are, and your name sums up that parable or represents it. In like manner every name in the Bible has a special meaning, representing certain faculties or conditions of the human soul.

The geography of the Bible is significant, too. Egypt, Palestine, Assyria, Babylon, the Mediterranean—all have symbolical meanings. Every river, mountain, lake, desert, etc. represents certain states of consciousness.

Numbers also are used to convey definite ideas and principles. I should point out that the number six—the six-pointed star of David—represents the Old Testament.

Six means labor. The Old Testament was founded on the commandments of Moses, which means hard work. It is an external thing but better than nothing. The New Testament expresses seven, and it is the movement from law to grace. Paul has a good deal to say about grace. When we understand the Jesus Christ teaching we are no longer under the law but are under grace.

And finally, the letters of the Hebrew alphabet are particularly significant and have a symbolic meaning that runs through the Bible. Jesus makes reference to this when he remarked, "One jot* or one tittle shall in no wise pass from the law, till all be fulfilled."

The Bible has a center line, a backbone as it were, that hangs upon two ideas, one in the Old Testament and one in the New. In the Old Testament it is the word ISRAEL. In the New Testament it is the name JESUS CHRIST. Israel in the Old and Christ in the New; one preparing the way for the other, and each complete and summarizing the other. They are major keys in the dramatic diagrams for living found throughout the Bible.

Israel in the Old Testament means a man and it means a nation, but more importantly is used symbolically to dramatize your life. Israel concerns your health, your job, your family, your finances, and your every personal problem. They are the things that are bound up with the story and the unfoldment of the history of Israel in the Old Testament.

The story of Israel began with Jacob, one of the most interesting characters in the Bible. There is something painfully familiar about Jacob. He is so very much like our own dear selves. He is not the saint or the mystic. He is every man, the man in the street, you and me. He was

---

* The smallest Hebrew letter.

selfish, made many mistakes, and did some outright sinning. But there is much more to Jacob than that, just as there is more to each one of us. In spite of all his shortcomings and mistakes, Jacob was uneasy in error. He was always yearning for the higher thing. He had a real desire to be better. Isn't that like ourselves? Isn't that the story of the whole human race? We get off the path, we have our problems, but through it all we know there is something better that we can aspire to.

And so the story of Jacob, as indeed the whole of the Bible, gives real clues to the handling of our life and our problems. We might say they are diagrams for living as we act and react in certain ways. The story of Jacob has all the charm of a fairy tale, yet it deals with cold reality, for Jacob was a real person; and his wrestling with the Angel is a great incident in the history of the human race.

Jacob was uneasy in error and that was his outstanding virtue. There is only one thing that can keep you out of the kingdom of God, out of health, happiness, and true success—and that is lying to yourself and refusing to face up to things. That was not one of Jacob's faults. He had made many mistakes, but he had prayed many times and had overcome them. Indeed, when Jacob was not doing wrong, he was praying! Does that sound like somebody you know?

The account begins with Jacob starting back for his own country. He had very much wronged his brother Esau. That sometimes happens in families. One brother takes advantage of another. Jacob, with the connivance of his mother, had stolen the "blessing" that rightfully belonged to Esau. Consequently, as Jacob started back with his family and servants and flocks and herds, he feared reprisals from his brother—the most natural thing in the world. Jacob had a guilty conscience.

Symbolically, Esau and Jacob, who were twins, represent the lower and the higher nature. Esau represents the lower, the animal nature that has to be redeemed and overcome by Jacob who represents the higher nature.

You may say, "That is very strange. Jacob was a very mean fellow, dishonest, selfish, cowardly. He was the reverse of everything we mean by a gentleman." That is true. Jacob was all these things and more. The Bible in presenting its characters does not try to cover up or gloss over the bad points just to give a good impression. That may happen with an author writing a biography of a well-known person. But not the Bible. It tells all about its characters, and it uses them to portray states of the human soul.

Esau means "red," the red earth. He stands for material man. But Esau was not really a bad sort. He was rough and materialistic. He might raise his fist and punch you in the nose, but you always knew where you stood. He was a rough, obvious kind of fellow.

We are told that the infant Jacob, as he was being born, grabbed hold of the heel of his brother Esau, the firstborn. The heel is always symbolic of the weak point in man. Achilles, the hero of *The Iliad*, had a vulnerable spot in his heel. He was held by the heel by his mother when she dipped him into the river, the waters of which made one invulnerable. A very convenient river to have! Where her hand held his heel, that spot was not affected by the water, and afterward he was conquered by being wounded in that exact place.

In the Bible, too, the heel stands for a weak spot and everybody has one, or two, or perhaps more. The heel is the part of the body that contacts the ground. Esau's weak spot was his love of material things, his willingness to sacrifice his inheritance for a mess of pottage prepared by his brother, Jacob.

So Esau stands for your material life, for your concept of yourself as a material being before you come into Truth. I didn't say before you come to church. I said "before you come into Truth." It is much easier to come into church than into Truth.

If you identify yourself in a purely human and material way—John Smith or Mary Jones, age forty-five, a father who drank and a mother who didn't love you, annual salary of $10,000 but unending indebtedness, unable to get about too much because of a weak heart, etc.—then you are Esau.

But Jacob, with all his faults, is the spiritual man. That is why Jacob is the Supplanter, which in Hebrew literally means "one who takes the place of another." This is symbolized in the Bible account by his catching hold of his brother Esau by the heel—Esau's weak spot. The spiritual idea supplants the material. It is a story of spiritual development. The material man, Esau, is supplanted by enlightened man who knows he is fundamentally a Prince of God with great potential spiritual power.

In the beginning, Jacob had great faults; but something happened to him—and that is the whole theme of the story. Jacob was changed more completely than any character in the Bible. In the long line from Adam to Jesus, some characters improved tremendously, some deteriorated terribly, but no one changed like Jacob. This is why he is so constructively important for us. He shows us the way for the return to God and freedom and harmony.

When we really know and understand Jacob he becomes the most consoling figure in the whole Bible.

There is not a fault that you may have that Jacob did not have in the strongest degree. There is not a weakness you would like to overcome nor a mistake you would like to rectify that could not be found in Jacob too.

But then something happened to Jacob. He had been away from his home in a foreign country. He turned and started back home, full of fear and trembling that his brother Esau would retaliate for the wrong Jacob had done to him. He feared not only for his own life, but also that of his family and servants, and the loss of his vast possessions. He knew that everything was at stake.

What did he do? Turn to God first? No. He did as so many of us do. He began to rearrange outer affairs. He divided up his flocks. He put the handmaidens in front— people who he thought did not matter very much. He put them first in the line of danger. Then he took the wife that he did not care for very much, Leah, and she was put in second place. And then the wife he cared for, Rachel, and his favorite child were put in the safe place. How like ourselves! We try to arrange a cavalcade so that the things that we set store by will be a little safer than the things we think we can spare.

Then he sent servants ahead with presents to appease his brother. He drew up elaborate plans so that all might not be lost. And that is what most people do. They write letters. They see people. They make inquiries; they run around, wearing themselves out. They do the outer things first.

Finally, Jacob, who deep down had a real longing for God, came to his senses. He decided to turn to God. The Bible says, "And Jacob was left alone." Read Genesis 32:24–32. There are only nine verses, but it is a literary masterpiece. "Jacob was left alone." A very telling phrase. When the great struggle comes you will always be alone in facing the problem. That is your test. At that time, seemingly encompassed by the terrors of hell, if you turn to God you are going to meet the wrestling Angel. It is something very worthwhile. You will have taken a great stride forward on the spiritual path, and you will find yourself a new man or woman.

Well, Jacob was left alone that night. Darkness or night is one of the great Bible symbols, meaning trouble and limitation. Struggles always come in the dark night of the soul, in blackness and despair. "And there wrestled a man with him until the breaking of the day." Later on we are told it was an Angel, but it seemed at first like a man. Our problems are never sublime. They always affect life here on the human plane. It is only later on when the thing is over that it takes angelic form, and we can look back upon the problem as a bad dream. The struggle lasted all night, symbolic of the fact that sometimes difficulties take a lot of prayer and treatment, until we see the dawn of a new day.

"And when [the Angel] saw that he prevailed not against him, he touched the hollow of [Jacob's] thigh." And the Angel said, "Let me go, for the day breaketh." And Jacob said, "I will not let thee go, except thou bless me." Jacob, with all his faults, had a real faith in the power of God. He would not accept anything less. He was almost exhausted, everything gone but his faith in God, but he would not let go.

When the dark hour comes and we have to struggle, seemingly alone, that is the time if we hold fast to the Truth, if we will wrestle with our idea of God—that is the time when we are going to get our closest link with God and take our greatest step forward.

And the Angel said unto him, "What is thy name?" And he answered, "Jacob." And with that the Angel said, "Thy name shall be called no more Jacob, but Israel: for as a prince hast thou power with God and with men, and hast prevailed."

The struggle was over; the problem was solved. Esau, his brother, good, generous soul that he was—rough, tough, coarse, crude, honest—forgave him, and Jacob was safe. But Esau could not have done this either if Jacob had not first met the Angel. Jacob's grasping the heel of his brother Esau at birth was prophetic of the fact that when Jacob was redeemed, he also redeemed Esau. The soul that is illumined, the soul that accepts God, redeems the body.

More important than this, Jacob knew he would never have to meet that problem again. As a result of this experience he came to realize the unreality of matter and the allness of God—or as the Bible says in its Oriental phraseology, "Thy name shall be called no more Jacob, but Israel."

Jacob had changed. He had a new name. As soon as you change yourself through prayer, your real inner name changes. Now, it is not simply a matter of changing your name. If you are Bill Brown or Mary Smith, changing your name would only upset the income tax people and the landlord, but it would not change the real you. You do not change the inner man by changing the outer name.

Jacob became Israel, and Israel is one of the most significant names in the Bible. It is the central idea that runs through all the Bible, beginning at the 11th chapter of Genesis with the call of Abraham, and ending with the Book of Revelation.

This is important because the Bible is full of promises to Israel and things that will happen to Israel. We are told, "Be fruitful and multiply. . . . kings shall come out of thy loins." Elsewhere it says, "Thy seed shall possess the gate of his enemies." People used to think these were material promises to the Jews, but obviously they are not, because it is now getting on to over four thousand years, and the Jews have never been a powerful nation in the material sense. Since the taking of Jerusalem in Old Testament times, they have nearly always been persecuted as a people.

In other words, these promises did not apply to Israel as a race of people. They are studies in consciousness and apply to all people who are seeking God. If you are really seeking God, not pretending to yourself or others, but really seeking God, then your seed, as the Bible promises, will possess the gate of your enemies. You will get your health, freedom, understanding, and true place.

The gate is the strategic point. This was especially true in the Old World where they had walled cities. Those who had possession of the gate, had possession of the city. It is relatively true in this age. For instance, the gates of New York City are the bridges and tunnels leading into the city. There are also gates to the world such as the Suez and Panama canals, the English Channel, and the Dardanelles, and that is why nations go to war over them.

In your personal life, the gates are the strongholds of consciousness. These are the sentinels we set up that allow certain ideas and beliefs to enter our minds. The Bible, in giving a kind of overall diagram for living, promises that if we will really put God first we will triumph over our enemies—those negative thoughts and conditions that come into our lives. God does not have to be the only thing in your life but He must be first. If you are honestly putting God first, then you are promised triumph. That is the covenant or agreement between God and man. Jacob becomes Israel.

Names are significant and this word *Israel* is one of the most important of all because the name Israel tells the story of the nature of God and man. That is why Jacob becomes Israel. He was the third in line: Abraham, Isaac, Jacob—body, soul, and spirit—soma, psyche, and pneuma.

Israel is made up of three syllables: *Is-ra-el.* First of all, *Is* means the feminine principle. *Is* came into the Bible from Egypt, from the goddess Isis. Isis was the mother goddess, the wife of Osiris. We must remember that the Hebrews had been in Egypt for several hundred years, and the Egyptians were the cultured people of their day. The more intellectual of the Hebrews, Moses among them, drank up all the education they could get. They learned from the Egyptians and naturally they used the Egyptian terminology.

So *Is* came from the name Isis. Isis has appeared in many guises. She was the Ishtar of the Babylonians, and then she appeared in Greece as Aphrodite, and later in Rome as Venus. The ancient Egyptians pictured Isis as a woman standing with the moon under her feet and the infant Horus in her arms. It was a kind of preview, an earlier expression of the picture we have of the Madonna and child.

We also get *Is* in Isaac. He too represents the feminine principle, and the feminine principle is always representative of the soul or mind. Isaac was receptive, reflective, introspective, a thoughtful type. In the Bible he is associated with wells. He was always digging wells. Wells and springs symbolize a contact with God, and represent the ever-new thoughts and ideas bubbling up into consciousness.

The syllable *Ra* in Israel comes from the name of the Egyptian sun god. He is that very much needed two-letter word we find so useful in modern crossword puzzles. *Ra* represents the masculine principle and is typified in real life by Abraham who is the man of action. Isaac represents the receptive state of mind while Abraham represents the executive state of mind, and we need them both.

When you are learning, studying, getting instruction from God, you must be receptive. You must be Isaac. You must be doing creative listening. But when you want to achieve something or do some healing for yourself or someone else, you must be Abraham. You must go forward in faith. You must be forceful and vigorous. When you are treating or making statements of truth you must be cocksure. It is no good saying, "God is the only Power—I guess!" That heals nothing. But if you say, "God IS the only Power," and you mean it, that is what heals. When Jesus said to himself, "God is the only Power," he meant it, and he opened the eyes of the blind and unstopped the ears of the deaf. We say it and hope for the best. That is hope; but it is not faith.

We need the two states of mind: the receptive when we are learning and meditating and getting inspiration, the executive when we are going out to do and dare and accomplish.

El, the third syllable of Israel, was the favorite suffix of the Hebrews for God. It comes from the Hebrew word *Elohim*—God Almighty, God in greatness and fullness. *El* means the union of the Father and Mother principles making the third. *El* always means God, in completeness, the trinity. When you go through the Old Testament, notice how many words end in *el.* For example, Bethel, which means the house of God, and El-Bethel, meaning God in the house of God.

It is interesting that the names given to the angels end in *el.* There are three of them mentioned: Gabriel, Michael, and Raphael. Raphael is not mentioned in the Bible proper, but is formed in the Apocrypha. Gabriel means man of God. When you get an inspiration, that is Gabriel. Even if it is only a flash, or a good idea, or a hunch, it means that you have gotten a sense of the presence of God. Gabriel comes to you from God. Michael means "What is of God? Who is of God?" We weight the problem and realize that it is not of God. We deny the evil, giving no power to it. Michael contends for the Truth, just as Satan and Michael contended for the body of Moses. We use the denial when fear comes to us or bad news arrives. We say, "What of this? Is this from God?" And when we realize that it is not, we deny it. We deny that it has any power over us. We deny that it can frighten us. We deny that there is any Truth in it. When we use the denial in that way, that is Michael in the Bible sense.

The third angel is Raphael, which means God is helping me. Raphael is always associated with healing. The poet Milton makes Raphael one of the central figures in *Paradise Lost.* The Hebrews always associated Raphael with healing; and tradition says that it was the angel Raphael who came down to trouble the waters at the pool of Bethesda where Jesus healed the paralytic. And I believe it was the angel Raphael with whom Jacob wrestled, the angel who blessed Jacob and saved his life—who changed his name from Jacob to Israel. After you have denied the power of evil or sickness or limitation of any kind, and you have gotten some sense of the presence of God, then you will have the *conviction,* "God is healing me; God is blessing this situation." That is Raphael.

El represents the spiritual side of our nature, and is typified by the regenerated Jacob. Jacob, the son of Isaac,

CHAPTER 3

Water, Women, and the Moon

T HE word "Bible" means "the books." It is physically a collection of books, but metaphysically it is far more. It is a great vortex through which flows wonderful spiritual power into the individual soul who reads it with understanding.

It is interesting to know how it came to be called the Bible. The name goes back to the early days of the Christian Era, but it had its origin long before that. It takes its name indirectly from the ancient town of Byblos. Slumbering peacefully in the warm sun of the eastern shore of the Mediterranean, Byblos is one of the world's oldest continuously inhabited cities. It prospered through the changing political structure of the ancient world by maintaining a neutrality in which it served as middleman in the vast Mediterranean trade. The Greeks, who purchased Egyptian papyrus from Byblos, immortalized the city's name by giving the diminutive *biblion* to the paperlike product imported from it. In time the term was applied to any book written on papyrus, and early in the Christian

Era the name was reserved for the Christian's most important book—the Bible.*

The Bible contains a wealth of pure history, but primarily it deals with spiritual things that cannot be fully stated in limited language. So it uses symbols, parables, and allegories, all of which were well understood by the men who wrote the Bible. They obviously expected the reader to see beyond the literal meaning to the real heart of the Bible.

In the Bible there are three basic meanings to every passage, meanings that are not contradictory but that are supplementary and complementary. The first meaning is the historical fact or bare statement. The same is true of the parables and allegories. For example, Jesus' parable of the Ten Talents, or the Pearl of Great Price, or any of the others; all have a more or less obvious surface meaning. Behind that meaning is a secondary meaning, which lies imprisoned in the statement. And there is a third meaning, which is the change brought about in the soul when the spiritual significance is really obtained and understood.

It is the secondary meaning with which we are concerned, and it is because this inner meaning cannot be put directly into ordinary language that the Bible uses symbol and allegory. It is in this inner meaning that we find great diagrams for living.

So, whether it be parable or actual historical fact, there lie behind these accounts great spiritual truths. It should be re-emphasized that the lives of such real persons as Abraham, Moses, Mary, and Jesus are all grand parables

---

* Gleaned from "Byblos, Middleman of History" by John Ballantine, published in *Aramco World*.

of what can and does happen to the human soul. Consequently, the Bible is full of spiritual symbols that, when understood, unlock the doors to the more abundant life.

One of the most important symbols, which runs all through the Bible from Genesis to Revelation, is the symbol represented by Woman. The Bible is full of women, good women and the other kind; pleasant women and rather unpleasant ones; wise women and foolish women; rich women and poor women; simple women and learned women; all kinds of women.

Woman is a continuing symbol throughout the Bible for this reason: Woman stands for the human soul. From a metaphysical point of view the Woman is not just Eve, or Mary, or Jezebel, or any particular person. Woman signifies the human soul—your soul—or as psychology expresses it, the psyche or mind. That is represented by Woman, and the history of Woman in the Bible is the history of your soul, and one of the keys to your destiny.

The soul is not the divine part of you. This divine part is the "I AM," "pneuma," which we will consider later. Your soul expresses itself as your personality, and that includes everything in the conscious and subconscious mind. So it is the changing personality, the psyche, that is represented by Woman in the Bible.

The whole of history is really the story of the human soul, always changing, either getting better or getting worse. It is a receptive thing—this constant change in your thought—as you either allow the spiritual power, the "I AM," to govern, or you let the lower self have sway. So, WOMAN IS THE SOUL.

Another important symbol for the human soul is Water, and Water and Woman are closely connected. Water in the Bible, from beginning to end, means the human soul—another facet of the human mind-representing mental movement. For instance, the Israelites had to cross water—first the Red Sea and later the Jordan—to get into the Promised Land. In other words, there had to be mental movement, a change in consciousness, before they could make their demonstration.

A third symbol for the soul is the Moon. The Moon represents the human personality with emphasis on the subconscious mentality that is the power behind the mental "throne." In *Romeo and Juliet*, Juliet says to Romeo: "O, swear not by the moon, th' inconstant moon." But they do. And of course the Bible says, "swear not at all." Woman, Water, and the Moon are all interrelated. The moon governs the water. Every drop of liquid on this planet answers to the moon twice a day. The ocean, the lakes, the coffee in your cup, and even every drop of blood in your body responds to the moon twice a day. If you should let a cup of tea or coffee stand for twenty-four hours, there would be a tide in it just as there is a tide in the Atlantic Ocean. Of course, it is too small to be observed or measured, but it is there nevertheless.

So this gives us an inkling of the nature of the relationship that exists between the cosmos and man. These three things, Woman, Water, and the Moon, mean the soul.

Eve, who appears in the allegory about Adam and Eve in the Garden of Eden, is the first expression of the soul in the Bible. The word "Eve" means life, or being, and your soul is your life or being here. It is derived from the word "Isis," the moon-goddess of Egypt. There is a wonderful old picture, found in many museums, of a woman with a child in her arms, and with the twelve stars around her head and the moon under her feet. It represents the goddess Isis whom the Egyptians called the Queen of Heaven. It is an idea far older than Christianity, teaching the truth about God and man, and the soul that has sought God and come through discouragement. Discouragement is one of the most powerful of "devils." It keeps the soul back almost more than anything else.

It was Eve who ate of the forbidden fruit, and as a result she and Adam got into difficulties and were driven out of Paradise. Adam in this parable represents the physical body. The word "Adam" means "red earth" or clay—the dust-to-dust idea. Now, the soul is the source of all your troubles. Nothing ever happens to your body that does not first happen in your soul or mind. If you are sick, that sickness was first in your mind, either because you accepted a prevalent belief with your conscious mind, or because it was lodged in your subconscious mind through previous negative thinking. Whatever appears in the body is first in the soul. The woman—the soul—eats of the forbidden fruit and then the trouble appears in the body and outer conditions.

So the first woman we hear about in the Bible is Eve. Then there is a whole procession of women in the Old Testament: Sarah, the wife of Abraham; Rachel and Leah, the wives of Jacob; Miriam, the sister of Moses; Deborah, the prophetess and "Judge" of Israel; Jezebel, wife of King Ahab; and many more. Then in the New Testament we come to the Virgin Mary, the soul who gives birth to the Christ child. That is a much different state of consciousness from the Eve state. Eve represents the soul in the ignorant or "not knowing" condition, the experimental condition. It tries this and it tries that, and because it tries evil as well as good, it gets into trouble. It is the mixed fruit that causes difficulty. If we are to avoid going from pillar to post, we must steadfastly abstain from evil, from the lower or negative thought, no matter how tempting the "fruit" may be, and cleave only to good.

The serpent that beguiled Eve is an old and complicated symbol that stands for limitation, enticement into limitation, the "easy" way. On the lower level it means difficulty, restriction, frustration, according to the many things occurring to the soul. The serpent comes to tempt the soul in some shape or form, and the Bible represents God as dramatically saying, "I will put enmity between thee and the woman, and between thy seed and her seed; it shall bruise thy head, and thou shalt bruise his heel." As we noted with Jacob, the heel represents the vulnerable spot in one's thinking, one's emotions, one's body, one's character. But of course, the heel is also the part that comes in contact with the ground and signifies that ultimately we shall crush the head of the serpent. The soul crushes the head of the serpent when you realize your spiritual character and refuse to be beguiled into seeking or taking the lower path with its temptations and deceptions.

Now, in the beginning the man is Adam, the red earth, because he believes what he experiences is the real thing. He thinks, "I am John Smith. I am forty years of age. I am a lawyer. I live in such and such a place. I have two children. I am a Methodist." But that is not the real man. That is Adam, the limited expression; while the true self is Divine Spirit. Always man is first the physical body; but later he recognizes that he is basically and fundamentally spiritual. Adam becomes the Christ. As Paul later says, "The first man is of the earth, earthy; the second man is the Lord from heaven." You must "be renewed in the spirit of your mind" by putting off the old man and putting "on the new man, which after God is created in righteousness and true holiness."

When the soul and the spirit become one with God, that is the mystical marriage, and any infidelity to that union is adultery, not marriage. The Virgin Mary symbolizes the virgin soul, but this does not necessarily mean an unmarried person. A married person can be just as spiritual as an unmarried person. You can have a pure mind no matter what state you are in. The virgin soul is the soul that has put God first and is completely concentrated on God—dutiful to family, friends, neighbors, business, etc.—but dutiful to God first. The virgin soul is first the bride and then becomes the wife.

Sometimes it happens that the soul feels it has fallen away from God. For days, weeks, months, or perhaps years it has been filled with peace and beauty, and then for some reason that fades out and is lost for a while. The Bible says, "left a widow," and a widow's state was a hard one in the Orient. Mystics call that "the dark night of the soul." That is a testing time when you wrestle with the Angel all night long, or perhaps night after night, until light comes again.

The most important thing in the long run is belief in the union with God. Infidelity really means lack of faith in God. It does not mean that you do not believe in the teaching of a particular church, or that you do not believe in the Thirty-nine Articles or the Westminster Catechism. It means you do not have faith in God to help you and teach you. In the Bible, adultery, infidelity, and idolatry are interchangeable terms. For this reason it is not in reference to the physical but in connection with the soul as "the bride of the spirit" that the terms are used. Do you see the symbolism?

Jesus was the first of the great teachers to put women on equality with men—the woman just as good as the man, her soul just as important—and she could do just as much right or wrong. The people around him in the area where he was brought up had regarded woman as simply an appendage of man. If he went to heaven, she went with him as part of his luggage! Jesus came forward and said no—woman had a soul of her own. He was the first to really teach that, although, unfortunately, his teaching was not carried out until very recent years. Even Paul had his reservations concerning women.

It has been a long and sometimes bitter struggle, but through the years women have found increasing freedom and equality with men. And it is because woman fundamentally represents the human soul that wherever and whenever women have been emancipated, both the standard of living and the spiritual welfare of the entire population have advanced.

The Bible handles its women characters in a complete and thorough manner. It speaks of a virgin prominently and frequently in the prophecies and throughout the story of Israel—the virgin daughter of Israel, etc. It speaks of woman as wife and spouse. It says that when you are really sincere in finding God, you will be no longer to me a servant but a wife, for "thy Maker is thine husband." God will not be your master but your husband. It speaks of the true wife and the woman not the true wife throughout the Old Testament. For instance, Abraham wed Hagar, the bond-servant of his wife Sarai. But Hagar was by no means the equal of Sarai, and their sons were not equal either.

There are many, many instances, then, of the wife, the spouse, the bride, and the mother, and sometimes as already stated, a widow. It even speaks of the soul as an adulteress. All these terms have a real and significant meaning.

Remember, when you read the Bible, you are reading an ancient, Oriental book, compiled for a population living under different conditions and needs, and above all, for a population that could neither read nor write. Consequently, many of its symbols are perhaps not in perfect accord with modern taste. We must take the Bible as we find it, and seek for the underlying meanings.

The Bible presents another condition of the soul in the person of Jezebel, a lady with a reputation. Jezebel was the daughter of Ethbaal, the King of Tyre. She married Ahab, King of Israel, and for many years wielded her evil power. She did everything she could to promote pagan rites and religion and to destroy the worship of the one true God. The Bible says, "There was none like unto [King] Ahab, which did sell himself to work wickedness in the sight of the Lord, whom Jezebel his wife stirred up." In her personal life she constantly entertained the heathen prophets of Baal and others, until it was common gossip of her "whoredoms" and "witchcrafts." In the exercise of her lust for power and her remorseless brushing aside of anything and everything that interfered with the carrying out of her evil designs, she was the veritable prototype of Catherine de Médicis.

Jezebel represents the soul that is completely given up to selfishness, sensuality, and material things. She came to quite an unpleasant end. She was thrown down from a high place. When one gets up on a high horse he finds himself in one of the most dangerous spots in the world.

A new king, Jehu by name, came to town to wipe out the wickedness in the palace. Jezebel went out on an upper balcony and shouted to him. He ordered that she be thrown down to the ground, and her body lay there

until the dogs devoured it, which was considered a very
bad end. Dogs in the Bible refer to pariah or scavenger
dogs, which are repulsive in every way. The story tells us
that the dogs devoured Jezebel, leaving only her skull,
the palms of her hands, and the soles of her feet. The
skull symbolizes the intellect. The palms of the hands
are diagrams of destiny, and the soles of the feet represent previous lives. In other words, Jezebel did not escape her destiny by dying. She would have to meet the
consequences of her wrongdoing elsewhere.

The left hand, in a manner, represents the "cards" you
start life with, and the way you handle them, the way you
play the game of life, is represented in the right hand.
People in the Truth movement usually find that the right
hand is better than the left because they make a consis-
tent effort to elevate their consciousness and thus spiritually improve their lives.

You cannot dodge your problems. You cannot dodge
the consequences of your thoughts and deeds. You have
to meet them, work them out and wipe them out by
prayer, realizing God sufficiently to clear them away; or
like Jezebel, you will be destroyed and will have to tackle
them in some other incarnation.

In contrast to Jezebel and all that she stands for, we
have the Virgin Mary. Mary represents the soul that is
centered upon God. It is the soul that is definitely saying, "Now, I am going to put God first and everything
else in my life is going to be secondary. I shall do my duty
but outside things will have to take second place. From
now onward, the thing that really matters is finding God
and developing my soul." The Bible calls that "the second birth" in some places, and that state is represented
by the Virgin Mary. She came from Nazareth.

All of these geographical names signify certain conditions that the soul may find itself in. These symbols are not fanciful. They are definite codes, just as an engineer finds certain symbols in a book dealing with engineering problems. Of course, you will find the Bible symbols appearing not only in the Bible but also in the old occult literature, in old folk stories, fables, and fairy tales. These symbols are repeated in literature, art, and architecture everywhere. Some of the New York buildings have them—at Rockefeller Center, for example. Go to the Metropolitan Opera and listen to any of Wagner's operas. Though he may not have been consciously aware of it, he was using this sort of symbolism in every one of his operas.

Nazareth has a meaning. It means "set apart." It does not mean going away into the desert and taking oneself out of the world. It means being *in* the world but not *of* the world. The Virgin Mary came out of Nazareth and the world of that day said, "Can any good thing come out of Nazareth?" Mary coming out of Nazareth means you must set your soul apart or the Christ child cannot be born.

The human soul finds itself in the condition where it is seeking for God because it is never really happy without God. And when the soul really becomes centered upon God, that is Mary.

The word "Mary" has two meanings. We have it in the form of the Hebrew word "Miriam," the sister of Moses, and we have it as "Mary," the mother of Jesus. One means "rebellion" or "insurrection," the rebellion of the soul against present limited conditions. The other meaning comes from "Marah" meaning "bitter," a struggle to escape from the limitation of self but not without bitter experience.

CHAPTER 4

"Man the Builder"

*For we know that if our earthly house of this tabernacle
were dissolved, we have a building of God, a house not
made with hands, eternal in the heavens.*

2 CORINTHIANS 5:1

W E have considered several important Bible symbols that give clues to our destiny. There is another outstanding symbol that runs throughout the Bible, and that symbol is the builder and buildings. The Bible speaks of man in many different occupations. Sometimes he is a fisherman, sometimes a farmer, a husbandman, a soldier. But always he is the builder because he is building his own soul.

The Bible is full of builders, and it also has a number of the most interesting buildings that are symbols of the human soul and the human body—psyche and soma. This is where we get our word *psychosomatic* medicine, which deals with the influence of the mind over the body in illness. Over the years the medical profession has gradually assigned a greater and greater role to the mind as the cause of disease. Someday it will understand that everything we find in the body, whether health or disease, is always the expression of something already in the mind or soul.

Your real identity, your real self, the Christ man, builds through your psyche or soul. Actually you are constantly building a new soul. As Paul says, "For we know that if our earthly house of this tabernacle were dissolved, we have a building of God, a house not made with hands, eternal in the heavens."

This body is not eternal at all. You get a new body about once a year; not exactly on your birthday, but your body is being renewed gradually all the time. The hair grows; a cut in the skin gradually heals, and various parts of the entire body are constantly being renewed. It was once thought that the body was completely renewed every seven years, but we now know that it is about every twelve months. The building materials are our thoughts. We build our lives all day long by the thoughts we think, the beliefs we accept, the feelings we entertain. Thought and feeling are the materials, and we are the builders. We build as individuals and we build as a race, and the thing we build manifests as our bodies and our world.

You have built your present body. If you want to know what sort of job you have made of it, just look in a mirror. That is what you have built. If you have poor lungs, they have been broken down by your thought and your emotions. Your home and occupation have been built by your thought. Indeed, all the conditions of your life have been built by the thoughts and feelings you consistently entertain.

Collectively as a race we have built the present conditions of the earth. The conditions and circumstances on this globe we live on are the outpicturing of the thoughts of mankind. Beautiful scenery is the outpicturing of man's understanding of beauty, while the squalor and meanness in other places is the outpicturing of man's belief in lack and limitation. Fire, flood, and famine are the outpicturing of the race consciousness. Tornadoes, cyclones, and earthquakes are all the expression of man's hatreds and fears, resentments and apprehensions. When these negative attitudes pass away from the human heart, the negative conditions will disappear too. For they are but the outpicturing of man's soul—not of the particular people who live in the regions affected, but of the whole human race.

Jesus was asked, on one occasion, a hard question concerning this. There had been several public calamities, and he was asked the question, "Why did this happen?" He answered, "Do you suppose the Galileans who were killed by Herod were any worse than the other Galileans? I tell you, no. Do you think that those upon whom the tower of Siloam fell, were worse than the others? I tell you, no. But unless you repent, you are all going to have trouble of one kind or another." To repent means to change your beliefs. Unless you change your beliefs, there will be difficulty.

What you believe is what you really expect to happen. You may say, "Oh no, I don't expect it to happen to me." But, as an example, if you have a strong belief in disease and think that there are ever so many diseases in the world and that any one of them could attack you and lay you low, then it is likely to happen to you at some time or another. When there is a strong belief that "there is a virus going around," there is also a strong possibility you will catch it. Why is the "common cold" so common? Because it is such a commonly held belief.

Thus, our conditions are "brought" to us by the kind of thoughts and feelings we build into our subconscious mentality, and our conditions are overcome or changed, by changing that mentality, by realizing that we are actually the builders. Thus do we build not only our individual consciousness, but we contribute our share to the race consciousness. Man is the builder.

There are a number of buildings in the Bible and they are exceedingly interesting when we realize that the Bible is the story of our unfoldment, containing diagrams for living. One of the very first building projects was Noah's Ark, the importance of which we will discuss later. Then there is the Tower of Babel, which I have discussed at length in my book *Alter Your Life*.* And there is that little ark in Egypt in which Moses was found floating on the Nile. This ark was a building of the simplest type in which the child was saved—the child who as a man led his people out of Egypt.

In this teaching you build an ark, or someone builds it for you, spiritually of course, in order that Moses—the Moses of your own consciousness—may bring you out of Egypt, out of your bondage. Moses got his people away from the oppression of Pharaoh, out of Egypt, parted the waters of the Red Sea, and got to the other side. These things may appear strange and unbelievable. But a new teaching is quite likely to sound strange. If you cannot accept it all at first, then accept as much of it as you can, and as you get spiritual understanding, you will accept more and more.

After the Israelites crossed the Red Sea, they did not at once enter Palestine, but they spent forty years wandering around in the "wilderness." In the Bible "forty" does

---

* Harper & Row, p. 84.

not mean a specific number, such as four times ten. It is a symbol meaning an indefinite time. This is the Bible's way of saying that the Israelites wandered about in the wilderness for an indefinite time before they could get to their Promised Land.

Why didn't they go straight to Palestine? It seems stupid of them that they did not immediately go to their objective. But what about ourselves? We know the Presence of God is there. We know that we have only to enter "the inner chamber" and trust God completely. Yet, do we do it? No, we do not. Instead of going straight into the Promised Land, we wander in the wilderness for an indefinite time.

This is where we are today, in the wilderness wandering about, and always with a ready excuse. "I need a little more time, or a little more treatment . . . When I have more understanding . . . Well, I'll start next week," and that sort of thing. There is always the willingness to postpone, instead of seizing the presence of God. That is our wilderness stage.

During their wanderings, the Israelites, because they basically believed in God and in prayer, created a tabernacle. It was not built of brick or stone, but it was a carefully built but movable tent or marquee. It could be taken up and carried away. It had been precisely built upon instructions that Moses received in the Mount. The tabernacle is the early concept of the "temple of the living God," which is the body temple. The pattern Moses received on the Mount was the divine diagram of man as God sees him. It is God's idea of man, God's perfect creation, and any departure from that pattern gives rise to sickness and lack of one kind or another.

This tabernacle was the first temple in which the Israelites held their services. On the march they folded it up and carried it about with them. It was intended to be only temporary until they settled down. In the Promised Land they expected to build a permanent tabernacle, which they did, the Temple of Solomon.

This is our present condition as a race, wandering about in the wilderness, not yet having built the new consciousness—the permanent tabernacle. Some people have had occasional demonstrations, instances of turning to God when fears and troubles have disappeared and things have gone right. But for the most part these demonstrations have been all too infrequent. As conditions change from time to time, we take the tabernacle with us because we too basically believe in God. (Just as many people would not be without a Bible in the house; yet they never take it off the shelf to look at it!) So in all our wanderings our tabernacle goes with us, not permanent but temporary. On the "march" the tent is taken down and folded up, and when the tent is folded up we cannot get into it to commune with God.

However, if you want to contact God, you positively must pause in the rush of things, in the wilderness of confusing thoughts and distressing ideas. You must come to rest, pitch your tent, and give attention to God. Many people will not do that. Like the Israelites, they remain in the wilderness and are knocked about considerably before they decide to make a bold move on the Promised Land.

That is what the Israelites did, and in the story some wonderful details are given. It is interesting and significant that Moses did not enter the Promised Land. He had done his job well, a truly herculean task. He had led the multitude of people across the wilderness. He had given them a body of law to help them regulate their lives. He had set down sanitary regulations to insure good health in that desert region. He had settled their dis-

putes, which was no mean task in itself. He had brought
them to where the Promised Land was in sight. His work
was done. As a reward for all this, he was translated and
lifted out of the picture. Moses was one of the handful of
men who did not die but made his translation direct.

Moses was the "law-giver." Knowledge of divine law is
absolutely imperative in our unfoldment. However, to
enter into our Promised Land, we require Joshua to lead
us. Joshua symbolizes the unfolding realization of the I
AM, the Christ indwelling.

So the Israelites were led into the Promised Land by
Joshua, whose name means "leader," "savior." And in
order to get into the Promised Land, the Israelites had to
cross water. In other words, they had to rise to a higher
state of consciousness. "Water" always means the human
psyche, and we have to transmute the human psyche or
soul—not to destroy it but to redeem it.

Elijah had a similar experience. Toward the end of the
career of this great prophet he was training Elisha to be
his successor. He wanted to give Elisha a final lesson.
They had gone to Bethel (house of God) and Jericho
(intellect) and they finally got to the Jordan. Elijah took
his mantle and smote the waters with it. The waters parted
and they crossed over on dry land to the other side. "To
strike with his mantle" meant to hold a strong conviction of Truth. There is no use taking off your overcoat and
hitting whatever or whoever is in front of you. It was Elijah's conviction that God would open the way for him.
That is "striking the water." Crossing water is a demonstration over yourself, a victory for yourself. If you overcome a difficulty or someone does it for you, you have
crossed the Jordan.

The Book of Revelation prophesies that the time will
come when there is "no more sea." That will be when

the human soul will have been entirely transmuted. So the Israelites "crossed water" in that they crossed the River Jordan. "River" means purpose, and the chief thing about rivers is that they are always going somewhere. A lake or pond just stands there. The ocean simply is. But a river is always moving. It says, "Excuse me, I can't stop now." So the River Jordan stands for a particular purpose, and that purpose has to be transcended and the Jordan crossed. The Israelites crossed it and entered the Promised Land.

Now the chief city of Palestine has always been Jerusalem. Jerusalem means "city of peace," and it stands upon a hill. In the Bible the hill or mountain means the uplifted consciousness. It is a symbol of spiritual power, and it means prayer. "Valley," on the other hand, stands for fear, sin, and limitation. Moses, Elijah, Jesus, and other leaders in the Bible were often going up into the mountains for contemplation and spiritual renewal.

In the middle of Jerusalem was a great rock—on top of Mt. Moriah. This is the place where, according to tradition, Abraham was going to sacrifice his son Isaac, his firstborn. The common belief was that if a man had a son, he had a better chance of getting to heaven. So Isaac meant everything to Abraham both here and in the hereafter. Even so he was ready to sacrifice him. And you will have to be prepared to go up on Mt. Moriah and sacrifice, or be willing to sacrifice, some of your most cherished beliefs before getting your contact with God.

The rock was the Rock of Zion, and when the Israelites settled down there, they proceeded to build a great building on that rock, the Temple of Solomon—the central building of the Bible. There were three temples eventually built on that spot. First, the Temple of Solomon, second, the Temple built under Zerubbabel, and the third, the Temple of Herod, where the apostles went. It is significant that the Temple was built on a rock, for a rock does not shift or change.

The Bible is a book of desert people.* The desert of the Bible is sandy, and one thing about that kind of desert is that nothing permanent can be built upon it. The sand is always shifting. If a building were erected, it would soon disappear. That is why these people used tents in the desert. When a permanent building was required, they traveled about until they found a rock. This is the symbol of the Christ Truth, changeless and eternal. So the Temple of Solomon stands for the regenerated soul, spiritual consciousness—that which is built upon a rock. All through the Psalms, for example, there is reference to God as the rock of salvation.

It is significant that David, whose name stands for Divine Love, was not allowed to build the temple. God had revealed to David that it was not he who should build the temple but his son Solomon, the man of peace. As long as you have to fight troubles—and you must fight them with divine love—you cannot build the temple. Before you can build the temple, the fight must be over and you must get some peace of mind. When you are in difficulty, spend much time treating yourself for peace of mind. Solomon has to build the temple, and he has to build it on a rock, the Christ Truth.

At the entrance to the temple two pillars were set up in the porch. Everyone going into the temple had to pass between them. The one on the right was called Jachin and the one on the left, Boaz. These names have great significance as diagrams for living. Jachin means "the One" and represents the mathematical unity of the cosmos,

---

* See "The Garden of Allah" in *Power Through Constructive Thinking* (Harper & Row).

Universal Mind, God. There is an old expression, older than Pythagoras who used it, that God geometrizes. In the Middle Ages when the mystics had to hide much of their teaching from persecution, they often used the word *geometry* for what we call metaphysics. Boaz, the other pillar, means voice and represents the creative Word, the Logos, which is what gives man power to change his conditions through recognition of the One Universal Principle—God.

There is another interesting thing about the temple. It was built in silence. Some of our modern skyscrapers are the most beautiful buildings in the world, but one could not say they are built in silence. But the Temple of Solomon, the great temple of spiritual consciousness, has to be built in silence—not in boasting, not in telling people how advanced one is—but in quietness and in confidence. It is built in the "secret place," in that change of consciousness that comes with contemplating God. That is when the temple goes up.

In the Bible, materials have a meaning aside from their literal designation. The noble material is stone, marble being the most refined kind of stone. Base material is brick. It is made of slime and clay, the red earth. The noble materials always mean the spiritual self, while the base materials stand for the human man, the lower self. The Tower of Babel, symbolizing confusion, is made of brick, but the Temple of Solomon is made of stone. Bricks are artificially made by man, but stone is "given" to us—dug out of the quarry, squared and made up with a great deal of painstaking work. When you get a stone building up, it stands, whereas the brick building is apt to crumble away, particularly the brick of Biblical times, which was pretty soft. So the Temple is made of stone, and it must be built by spiritual thought and not by willpower or by sitting down and planning the arrangements.

A collection of buildings becomes a town or city, and in the Bible a city means the whole consciousness. Jesus used this simile when he said, "A city that is set on an hill cannot be hid." In other words, an outstanding consciousness is felt and recognized by everyone.

Your consciousness is made up of various "buildings." For instance, your physical body, your home, your job, your investments, your friends, your hobby, your church— all these different departments of your life are symbolized in the Bible as the buildings in a city. They are the outpicturing of the buildings that you have built in your "city," your consciousness.

The Bible has much to say about cities. The main city is of course Jerusalem, the Holy City, and Jerusalem, as we have seen, means the city of peace, the habitation of peace. Jerusalem represents the consciousness that has found the peace of God.

Jericho is another city mentioned prominently in the Bible. It was there that Joshua came upon what to human thinking seemed an insurmountable obstacle. It was a completely walled city. A walled city represents the consciousness that is closed to spiritual ideas. However, the Israelites always put God first. They were a praying people and so was their leader. Under divine guidance Joshua found a way that someone on the strictly material level of consciousness would not have thought of. He was told to have his army, along with the priests bearing the tabernacle, march around the city every day for six days. Six symbolizes labor—the six days of creation—the six steps to Solomon's throne—the six "steps" to demonstration. On the seventh day they marched around seven times, and seven always represents spiritual fulfillment, mission accomplished, demonstration made. The Israelites shouted and the priests blew on their rams' horns, and the walls came tumbling down.

Jericho means "moon town," and as we have seen, the moon stands for the subconscious mind. The subconscious mind has to be "subdued," to be redeemed by being spiritualized.

Two other towns in the Bible that are well known are Sodom and Gomorrah, which are particularly noted for their wickedness. Fire and brimstone were rained down on the cities, destroying the inhabitants. And, of course, this is an apt description of what happens to the consciousness given over completely to sensuality.

And then there is the little town of Bethlehem where Jesus was born. Bethlehem means "the house of bread," which in the Bible represents divine substance. This is the coming into consciousness of the Wonder Child.*

There are many other cities in the Bible representing various facets of the human consciousness. But ultimately there will be the New Jerusalem, which is not built out of clay from the ground or stone from the quarry, but comes down from heaven complete and perfect. That city is described in chapter 21 of the Book of Revelation. This is one of the supreme diagrams for living. It is a wonderful description of spiritual consciousness.

The Book of Revelation is a most exciting and amazing book, and as the years go on, it reveals more and more of its treasures, as the human consciousness expands and understands more. Revelation is intended to show the progress of the human soul as it climbs the spiritual ladder, and in that sense it is prophetic. It tells us what will

_____
* See "The Wonder Child" in *ibid.*

happen if we do certain things. We foolishly make all kinds of trouble for ourselves, and for the other fellow, but that was not God's intention.

We have to love life. We have to be interested in ourselves—and anyone who is not, has lost the savor of life. This is not the same thing as being selfish. If we love life and are interested in ourselves in a spiritual sense, we are interested in the quality of our thinking. We are interested in bringing it into harmony with Divine Love. We want conscious union with God so that we have a greater awareness of good in our lives. Chapter 21 of Revelation tells us a good deal about doing this by describing in the symbolical language of the Bible a wonderful city, the celestial city, a principality in which you are the prince, for this is your very own consciousness.

People who have taken the Bible literally have thought that it is describing a real city, like one might describe New York or London. But the Bible writer never intended that his description should be taken literally. For instance it says, "The city lieth foursquare, and . . . the length and the breadth and the height of it are equal." There never was and never will be a city that could be as high as it is wide or long. This is purely symbolic.

The writer gives us another clue in the next verse. He says that the angel "measured the wall thereof, a hundred and forty and four cubits, according to the measure of a man." And of course that means a woman too. It is the measure of the spiritualized consciousness, and each one's measurement will be different, depending upon how much he has advanced mentally and spiritually. John is expressing the idea that as you merge the mental and spiritual, things begin to change in your life, until at last you find spiritual union with God, the mystical marriage.

In this sense, the angel is always measuring the walls of your city, but in the beginning the measurement will not add up to one hundred and forty-four cubits because that is the ultimate, the city foursquare, the perfect thing. Twelve times twelve equals one hundred and forty-four. Twelve in the Bible and in all occult literature stands for corporate completeness, the thing the human race is striving toward, whether it knows it or not. But it is incumbent upon those who know it to work toward that goal.

In the beginning, people think and act on a minimum level, just getting by, having their ups and downs—probably more downs than ups. Then things begin to change when they fill their minds with great ideas from the Bible and from other uplifting literature. They meditate more and more on spiritual things. They let new ideas and inspiration flow in. They definitely seek divine guidance. They develop new attitudes and approaches to their problems, and they find their lives becoming more fruitful and meaningful.

The Bible account symbolizes all this by saying, "I saw a new heaven and a new earth . . . and there was no more sea." The sea represents the mental aspect of your nature, the subconscious, and as you begin to people your celestial city with new, vibrant, dynamic ideas, you are redeeming the subconscious—a thing that psychiatrists and psychoanalysts strive for in their patients. People often spend hours on the psychoanalytic couch trying to release deep-down negative ideas, mental blocks, repressions, and conflicts. But each one can do this spiritually and with less effort if he will make it a habit to accept only constructive and positive ideas and deny the power of anything negative.

Little by little we are building a new heaven and a new earth. And the Bible makes certain promises about that process. It says that "God shall wipe away all tears." That is good news, is it not? God will take away all grief, all suffering, all regret. God will wipe out old hurts and scars of the past. Many people have been hurt or disappointed in the past, and although they may not be actively grieving today, there is a scar and that scar prevents their getting complete peace of mind. Again it is a question of redeeming the subconscious.

The account goes on to affirm, "There shall be no more death." When you get right down to it, how many of us believe that? The Bible is not only speaking of physical death, which Jesus overcame. It is alluding to the death of hope and courage and faith and desire. To emphasize the point it continues, "neither sorrow, nor crying, neither shall there be any more pain." And that of course includes mental pain, sorrow, bereavement, deep remorse for some mistake, deep depression, melancholia. No more pain of any kind, "for the former things are passed away."

The Bible is saying that as you take into consciousness the constructive ideas, God will wipe away the negative thing. God will break down the barriers of doubt, defeat, frustration, and conflict.

The greatest mistake man makes is fear, which of course is a lack of faith. Fear prevents us from taking that next important step. Fear makes us distrust our fellow man. Fear sets group against group and nation against nation. When fear creeps in and takes possession, as we give the right of way to doubts and anxieties, we have begun to wreck the celestial city. When fear creeps in, faith flies out the window. Yet faith is the very cornerstone of all enterprise. Faith is the factor that gives the impetus of conviction to a thought and thus impresses the thought upon our subconscious as a conclusion that must be manifested in the material world. It sets up a blueprint for accomplishment, as it were. But when you begin to lose your faith, you are really saying to your subconscious, "I have now placed my faith in the negative. I have placed my faith in failure." Your subconscious takes it for an order and you begin to reap negative results. You have stopped building the celestial city.

Another great human mistake is a reluctance to let go of yesterday. That is why this chapter stresses "Behold, I make all things new." There is probably not a more important text in the whole Bible. Without newness of ideas, without newness of thought, there can be no progress either in the individual or in the race of mankind.

We have to let go of yesterday. Experience is only something to learn from, something to capitalize on, to lead us into a greater awareness of good. You may say, "There was a lot of good in yesterday. I found a lot of happiness in some of the things I did." Of course there was a lot of good in yesterday. But you cannot really hold on to the past, unless you want to miss your good today. Let go of the past, good or bad, and you will find something ten times as good will come into your experience. "Behold, I make all things new." And this means you, no matter who you are. It matters not what you are or what mistakes you have made, God looks to the heart and this is His promise to you: "Behold, I make all things new."

There is a verse in this chapter that is very well known, and it gives the reason for the fulfillment of all these promises. It says, "He that overcometh shall inherit all things; and I will be his God, and he shall be my son." Overcometh what? Overcometh fear, anxiety, and error. And the account goes on to say that if we do not do this we are going to have all kinds of trouble. That is not a threat. The Bible never threatens. It is merely stating the law. It is giving us another diagram for living.

It refers to the fearful and the unbelieving, and it lumps them with a lot of unsavory characters and says they shall have their part in the lake that burneth with fire and brimstone. This is a very good description of the lives of men and women who are filled with fear and anger and resentment, or overwhelming carnal desires, and are trying to live without God. Yet people have interpreted this text as meaning this is what happens to people when they die and go to hell. And they say, "The Bible calls this the second death."

But this has no more to do with physical death than when Jesus was asked by Nicodemus concerning his teaching. He said, "Except a man be born again he cannot see the kingdom of God." It had nothing to do with physical birth. Thus, here in Revelation, it is not talking about something that happens after death. It is the description of a kind of hell people go through in this life, and very often it is not only the second death but the third and fourth!

Revelation, and thus the Bible, ends on a high note. It brings in gold and all kinds of jewels in describing the celestial city—your consciousness. It says that the city has twelve gates, and as we have seen, twelve means completeness. The whole human race is going to be saved. How soon? That depends upon humanity, but sooner or later the whole race will understand the spiritual ideal and put God first. In the meantime, any individual who wants to can begin to do it for himself.

We are told the twelve gates were twelve pearls. Of course we know of the "pearl of great price." It is the one thing that is desirable above all others, the Presence of

God Himself, the true knowledge, the spiritual idea. Other precious stones mean other things. The sapphire means Divine Truth, the diamond means unchanging principle, the ruby means Divine Love, the emerald means Divine Life; and the pearl means the Presence of God.

This is emphasized by saying the whole city is pure gold. Gold symbolizes the omnipresence and all-power of God. It means that God can do anything at any time. He does not have to prepare or arrange. He is not concerned with conditions. It makes no difference to Him how long you have had some ailment, or that the world calls it incurable. It makes no difference to Him that you have made a fool of yourself and messed everything up; or what your age or any other condition may be.

Revelation is an amazingly detailed description of the celestial city—your consciousness. And your consciousness is the measure of your life.

CHAPTER 5

Turning the Tide of Trouble

And Noah walked with God.

GENESIS 6:9

THE story of Noah and the Ark is one of the most important stories in the whole Bible, and I suppose it is one of the best known. People who know very little about the Bible at least know the story of Noah and the flood. Why is the parable of Noah and the deluge so important? Because it is the story of our lives. It is another diagram for living, containing tremendous psychological and metaphysical truths. It shows us the way to overcome the larger difficulties that come along.

Actually, there is some historical foundation for the story because in the history of the world there have been several great inundations. One of these occurred in the long, long ago when Atlantis, a vast continent in the South Atlantic, was submerged, destroying a great civilization. In the same way the Mediterranean Sea was created by an earthquake, and by a flood that swept through what is now the Straits of Gibraltar. The Sahara desert was once the bed of an ocean, as was also the southwestern portion of the United States. In the Grand Canyon nature has given us a living picture of what happened there in the last five million years. The eroded sides of the canyon reveal embedded marine fossils, indicating that this area, now some 8,000 feet in elevation, was once underwater. One of these great floods is what lies behind the legend of Noah and the Ark.

The Bible account begins, "God saw that the wickedness of man was great in the earth, and that every imagination of the thoughts of his heart was only evil continually. And it repented the Lord that he had made man on the earth, and it grieved him at his heart." Our fundamentalist friends used to think that God Almighty made man as an experiment and that because he turned out badly, God was disappointed and very cross. However, God does not experiment. Man may experiment like an Edison, to find out something. God does not need to find out anything because God is all knowledge. God cannot use deductive logic. God could not be grieved at heart.

The Lord in this text means the Divine Spark in man himself. Because we have the Divine Spark in us, we never fully accept evil. Fear comes to people, giving rise to crime and sin, and things go from bad to worse. Because the divine spark is there we are rebellious against evil and limitation. Thank God for that. Rebellion against evil is a splendid thing. It has been said, "Rebellion to tyrants is obedience to God." What could be more of a tyrant than the laws we make for ourselves and the consequent limitations with which we surround ourselves. The name "Mary" means rebellion—insurrection against limitation—and Mary becomes the Mother of the Christ child.

So the very thing that makes you discontented, "I want no more illness . . . I am not going to put up with it . . . I ought not to have this lack or work that I hate," is the Christ power coming to you and urging you to change things. "Here I am on this earth surrounded by fear and limitation. I am not going to put up with this wickedness. I am going to change it." That is the Lord God, Jehovah, repenting that He had made man. So He instructs Noah to build an ark—a way out of the difficulty.

The thing that is important in the story of Noah and the Ark is the spiritual meaning underlying it, for it is a parable to illustrate great spiritual truths. It is built around a man who is wise and who is always praying. Always you will find in the Bible that when a man overcomes some difficulty, he is a man who prays. His Bible is open and thumbed; he does not keep it on the shelf. He prays. Daniel, you may remember, used to pray three times a day. Moses was a great pray-er, so was Abraham. Jesus spent whole nights and days in prayer. All these people gave much time to the search for God; and in this parable, Noah was one of them. Noah, of course, represents every man. He stands for your spiritual intuition, the Divine Spark within you.

The Ark is one of the most remarkable structures mentioned in the Bible. It was a big ship and it represents the state of mind that you build when there is trouble around. Instead of accepting the trouble, or giving way to it, or thinking it inevitable, or trying to run away from it, you build yourself an Ark, a mental sanctuary of true thought.

In the parable, things began to go wrong in the world. There was much wickedness. People had been thinking wrongly and behaving badly. People were jealous of one another, and hating and killing one another. A great deal of fear was generated as their faith in God ebbed away. They were carrying on in a general way pretty much as the "enlightened" Christian generations have been doing since the time of Jesus.

Noah was one of those few individuals who walked with God, who realized the presence of God and the Power of God, and he sensed the coming of trouble. You may not always get a warning when there is impending danger because you are usually too much "on the run," but always the divine self tries to send that warning through. Noah foresaw this trouble and went to work making the Ark.

His friends and neighbors thought he was a fool. "Whoever built a boat in the middle of dry land?" They laughed and poked fun at him, "Think it's going to rain a little, do you, Noah?" When you have a divine leading, you will surely lose it if you listen to other people, if you allow yourself to be dissuaded. If you have a purpose and a plan, especially if it comes from God, there will be plenty of people to tell you how foolish you are. "Oh, I tried that and dropped it long ago . . . I found it wasn't any good." That sort of discouragement. But Noah went right on shaping the timbers, and finally finished the Ark.

Now, if Noah had not been a man who walked with God, one who did not get direct inspiration, he would have waited until the trouble arrived. Then he might have been tempted to build a breakwater, or a levee, or a big house on stilts. Or he might have tried to run around throwing lifesavers to the people. But none of these things would have been of any use in the rush of trouble that engulfed the world. The job was too big for such limited thinking. Fighting such a vast sea of trouble would have been merely a waste of time. Under divine guidance Noah built a boat that floated above the trouble.

Water, as we know, means the human soul. This flood of water is representative of our daily life with our fears, our problems, our difficulties. For instance, if you are threatened with a fatal disease and the doctor has said, "I am afraid there is no hope," then the waters are on the face of the earth as far as you are concerned. The great deluge has come upon you. If you are facing financial ruin, then the great flood waters are on the face of the earth. If you are terribly disappointed and feel abjectly let down by someone you love or esteem highly, then the waters are on the face of the earth. Your only hope is to build an Ark and get into it. When you do not know where to turn, that is the time you must get into the Ark. That is what Noah did.

A remarkable thing about this Ark that Noah built—there was only one window in it. It was not a little porthole on the side of the ship. And it wasn't a skylight. Noah was preparing for heavy rain and he probably had had some experience with skylights and how leaky they can be. The only window was up under the roof as high as it could be put. Why was the window there? Because of what I call the Golden Key.* It was constructed in this way so that Noah and those with him in the Ark would be obliged to look up at the sky. Up! That was the only way they could look out. In this way they could not look around at the flood and fill themselves with more fear.

The Golden Key tells us to think of God instead of the problem. Yet we know the itching tendency to have a peep to see how the flood is getting on. Praying one minute: "God is the only Presence and the only Power." And the next minute: "Six inches higher, no demonstration yet."

---

* See "The Golden Key" in *Power Through Constructive Thinking*.

Then: "God is the only Presence here now," and then back to the difficulty, "It's gone up another foot. Things are getting worse." That is how some people seek spiritual help, checking up on all their aches and pains!

You must not keep looking at the troubles that surround you. You must look away from them. You must rise up in consciousness. What most people do in the face of a dilemma is to say, "Oh, I just know we'll never survive this! . . . There's no way out now . . . Why did we ever get involved?" That kind of talk. Like Noah, you must steadfastly turn away from the trouble and look only at the "sky." In other words, you must elevate the consciousness through scientific prayer, through practicing the presence of God.

When you are in difficulty, turn away from it and practice the presence of God. Contemplate God. Cease to grovel in your sins. There are sects and movements that encourage people to talk about their sins but this is a mistake. Talking about them only roots them more firmly in the subconscious and makes them that much more difficult to eradicate. Make your peace with God. Turn away from the flood.

There are all sorts of interesting and significant details in the story of the Ark. For instance, Noah had three sons. Noah and his three sons make four. This suggests a parallel with the Four Horsemen of the Apocalypse.* Noah is the "rider" on the white horse. He represents the spiritual self. Shem, Ham, and Japheth are the other three "horsemen," representing the body, the intellect, and the feeling nature. Always the Bible is telling us about our own make-up, so that we may have peace and harmony and health and spiritual development. "Man know thyself."

---

* See "Four Horsemen of the Apocalypse" in *Alter Your Life*.

Noah and his three sons brought their wives along, signifying the balance of the male and female principles, that is, the knowledge and feeling aspects. The person who is all feeling with little intelligence is just an emotional fool. And one who is merely intellectual without feeling is lacking the proper balance, and the full expression of his life will be curtailed in one way or another.

And then, the part of the story that always delights children is the bringing of all the animals into the Ark. "Of every clean beast thou shalt take to thee by sevens . . . and of beasts that are not clean by two. . . ." I imagine that if some modern religious teachers had written the story, they would have left out the unclean animals. However, every human being is full of clean and unclean animals. That is why the Bible puts them in the Ark. The mistake is to try to get into the Ark with only the clean animals. The unclean animals must also be brought in and redeemed.

All these animals represent the various instincts, faculties, propensities, and powers of man. The unclean animals are faculties and powers we have not yet redeemed. They are sensuality, avarice, jealousy, covetousness, fear, etc. These are the things that have wrecked and ruined so large a number of people who have tried to leave them out of the Ark and have failed. The unclean animals are in twos, meaning the positive and negative aspects, and you have to redeem the negative side by realizing the positive and constructive until the negative fades out and thus is redeemed.

The clean animals are our spiritual faculties that we already have redeemed by using them for good. There were seven each of the clean animals because the number seven in the Bible signifies spiritual completeness, and of course this refers to the things in ourselves that we are using toward wider expression and divine achievement. The clean animals are the good in us, the love, wisdom, understanding, and unselfishness.

Our thoughts are very well expressed by animals. Some thoughts are creeping-on-the-ground thoughts. The thoughts, "I can't do it . . . I am not strong enough . . . I am too old." These thoughts creep on the ground as the serpents and snakes do. And then there are other thoughts that soar in the air: "I believe in God so I can and I will . . . I can overcome this thing . . . Nothing I have to meet is as strong as God in me." So the creeping things on the ground and the birds of the air went into the Ark. So did the cattle and the beasts of the field—our ordinary, everyday thoughts—useful thoughts like cows and sheep, very useful bread-and-butter thoughts, but not very exciting. Finally, there are the wild beasts, thoughts that fling discretion to the winds. So all the beasts in the Ark express things that are within ourselves.

Now, the rain came down and the flood covered the whole earth, and I am sure that a great many of you have experienced that "flood" at least once in your life when you could not see a way out and all seemed hopeless. So it was with Noah and those in the Ark.

After forty days Noah opened the window. Notice the number here again. In the Bible "forty" means an indefinite length of time, long enough to accomplish a certain thing. With the window open what did Noah do? He did what so many people do. He sent out the raven. We make still more trouble for ourselves by sending out the wrong thought. It is useless to send out the raven over the flood because the raven means negative thought. That idea is expressed in Poe's poem, "The Raven"—

"quoth the raven 'Nevermore!'" That raven may be criticism of others or self-criticism: if only I hadn't done such and such a thing. Or it may be self-pity, indignation, hatred. The two most deadly forms of the raven of wrong thinking are resentment and domination.

At any rate, Noah sent out the raven and of course nothing was accomplished. It simply went to and fro, back and forth, round and round—still the same problem, and Noah fell down lower than he had been before. Then seven days passed, again a complete cycle of consciousness working further to overcome that raven action.

Then Noah took the dove and sent her out. The dove represents a sense of peace. He treated, as we say; he rose in consciousness; he prayed. But he did not make his demonstration immediately, and seven more days went by. Many of us would have given up. We would have said, "What a fool I was to even hope." However, Noah, the rider of the white horse, went back again undaunted. If you will refuse to be intimidated by the difficulty, you will win. He worked seven days longer and sent out the dove again. And then we come to one of the most dramatic touches in literature. It is equally as dramatic as that passage in Defoe's *Robinson Crusoe*, when Crusoe, after weeks of loneliness and some despair of ever seeing another human soul, sees, not the person, but footprints in the sand. In this story of Noah the drama is the return of the dove with a little green olive leaf. In the evening—after a day's work—the dove returned to Noah, "and, lo, in her mouth was an olive leaf plucked off: so Noah knew that the waters were abated from off the earth." Then, after another seven days, he sent forth the dove again, "which returned not again unto him any more." The demonstration was made.

Put yourself in Noah's place. For days and months he had seen nothing but water. He had prayed and worked on his consciousness to raise it above the difficulty, and nothing seemed to change. Even after he had gotten some sense of peace concerning the problem and he had sent out the dove, there seemed to be no change in his condition. But persistence in prayer, and sustained knowledge that so long as you remain in the Ark of your spiritualized consciousness no harm can come to you, finally bring results. And so the return of the dove means the realization you get of the presence of God as the result of your prayer and meditation. When you realize at last that you have contacted God, you receive the glad tidings, the olive branch.

The olive branch is an important symbol to the American people because on the Great Seal of the United States, the eagle holds an olive branch in his claw. The men who formed the Constitution of the United States, the men who wrote the Declaration of Independence and put it into effect, and later ordered and designed the Great Seal, were men in many instances inspired without their conscious knowledge, and these symbols were woven into the fabric of the beginnings of this great nation.

The eagle's head is shaven to symbolize man's direct contact with God. The eagle holds the olive branch in his claw to symbolize that the American republic was created to bring this truth to the world, and that the American people, as well as all other nations, who accept this teaching have the power of getting their peace and their divine fulfillment. If you accept the truth and hold to it, you can send out the dove from the Ark, and after seven, or twice seven, or three times seven, it will come back bearing the olive branch.

After the waters had subsided there appeared a rainbow in the sky. The great catastrophe was followed by God's lovely gift of the rainbow. What could be more beautiful? And with a rainbow there is that feeling of newness that comes after a storm; a sense of joy and aliveness.

"And God said, This is the token of the covenant which I make between me and you and every living creature that is with you, for perpetual generations. I do set my bow in the cloud, and it shall be for a token of a covenant between me and the earth." Here is a definite promise, and a promise in the Bible means spiritual law. There is no end to the rainbow, and science tells us that you will never find the end of the rainbow outside because the rainbow is in the eye of the beholder. The Christ way out is in our own consciousness.

The rainbow is a symbol similar to the many-colored coat of Joseph, and represents the etheric body. It is the human aura, depicted in many religious paintings as a halo around the head. Your etheric body is colored in accordance with your habitual thoughts. Some people can actually see it—those who have etheric vision. When you are obtaining spiritual development and giving your time daily to prayer and meditation, you give it the most beautiful colors. When man has done sufficient spiritual work to destroy the flood and bring back the dry land, then he has achieved that coat of many colors that is spoken of here as the rainbow.

The following chapter in Genesis refers to Noah's getting drunk on wine. This has to do with the "profanation of the mysteries." It was not until Jesus did his work that the world was ready for this teaching. Before the time of Jesus it was forbidden to give out the sacred knowledge. That cannot happen today, but it is possible to use this Truth teaching not to contact God, not to serve humanity, but merely to get things. If you use this knowledge just for selfish ends, you will defeat your purpose and only harm yourself. Of course we need things, many things. Jesus knew this and that is why he went to pains to say, "Your heavenly Father knoweth that ye have need of all these things. But seek ye first the kingdom of God, and his righteousness; and all these things shall be added unto you." To go out only for the loaves and fishes is "profanation of the mysteries" in the modern sense.

The story of Noah and the Ark is a perfect diagram of the technique for handling a large problem, a rush of trouble. Noah represents our spiritual self, and the Ark symbolizes the state of mind we build when we see the problem or the trouble coming. Instead of accepting the difficulty or giving way to it, or letting it frighten us, or thinking it is inevitable, or trying to run away from it— we build an ark, a mental sanctuary, a quiet state of mind, by prayer. We build what, in this teaching, we technically call a state of consciousness. In that consciousness fear will have little power so long as we remain in the ark.

In that ark you continue in quietness, confident that the demonstration is being made. You refuse to look at the flood and thus fill yourself with fear. You refuse to send out the raven of dark, negative thought. You wait for the dove of peace to come into your soul. In the meantime, you continue in prayer. It may require a few days of prayer, or even weeks, but eventually you will get your sense of peace. That will be the "seven" days, and that will be the end of a problem you will never have to tackle again.

CHAPTER 6

The Called, the Chosen, and the Faithful

*And it shall come to pass, when Pharaoh shall call you,
and shall say, What is your occupation? That ye shall
say, Thy servants' trade hath been about cattle from our
youth even until now, both we, and also our fathers: that
ye may dwell in the land of Goshen; for every shepherd is
an abomination unto the Egyptians.*

GENESIS 46:33, 34

A NOTHER diagram for living is hidden in the symbol of the shepherd and his sheep. In the Bible, you take on many occupations. Sometimes you are a day laborer, sometimes the lord of the vineyard; sometimes you are a weaver, sometimes a fisherman. However, no matter how many different occupations you undertake, before you become the gardener of your own soul with conscious spiritual evolution, you are destined to become a shepherd. All these various occupations represent states of mind, and the Bible encourages you to become a shepherd because sheep mean thoughts and a shepherd keeps his thoughts.

Some of these striking symbols lose a little of their power in the modern world because so many of us live in the cities. But in ancient times sheep were as common a sight as taxicabs are to us, and of course the shepherd was a very familiar figure. That is why Jesus so frequently referred to the shepherd and his sheep. Sheep are thoughts and you are a shepherd—either a good shepherd or just a hireling—and the kind of thoughts you keep will determine the kind of life you have. If you harbor thoughts of anger, bitterness, and resentment, you cannot expect to have a life of peace and joy and harmony. On the other hand, if you keep your thoughts on a positive and constructive level, then you are going to demonstrate in accordance with that.

Beginning with the story of Cain and Abel, the idea of the shepherd runs all through the Bible. The story, like that of Adam and Eve, is of course an allegory. This point needs to be stressed, for Cain and Abel present another stumbling block to those who take the Bible literally. The heckler's question, "Who was Cain's wife and where did she come from?" is irrelevant when we know that the story is not history but metaphysical symbolism expounding spiritual Truth.

This wonderful allegory of Cain and Abel is really a dialogue between the material belief, which is Cain, and the half-belief of mind-over-matter, which is Abel, arguing with the Lord, which means the Truth of Being. Abel is just beginning to learn the power of thought and thought control. He does not yet have the understanding to rely completely upon his intuitive nature and disavow any belief in the power of matter. And so he allows the intellect to take over. Cain kills Abel.

Cain was a digger of the ground. He believed there was a separate, hard ground outside in which he had to dig and sow and fertilize and cultivate, and then wait a while for results. He believed he had to go through all that toil and servitude. Always the intellect points out limitations. Always it says, "No, not quite yet, better not." It always finds difficulties in things, and differences between people. Above all, it says, "It is too good to be true." It is because we allow the intellect to rule us that we have to earn our living by the sweat of our brow.

On the other hand, Abel was a keeper of sheep. In the Bible, as we have just seen, sheep always mean your thoughts, and so to be a shepherd means that you are beginning to control your thoughts. That is splendid but it is only the beginning. The Egyptians hated a shepherd, which is the Bible way of saying that inharmony hates thought control because thought control begins to destroy inharmony. Your arthritis, your quarrel, your bad temper, your fear, your regret, or your remorse—these things hate thought control because thought control is going to eradicate them. So Cain slays Abel.

Abel is the state of mind that says, "Yes, matter is there. There are germs; there are depressions, etc., but I think I can overcome it. I can pull myself off the ground by my bootstraps if I pull hard enough." But you cannot do that because as long as you believe that there is a separate power in the outer thing you cannot control it. It will beat you at the finish. Cain will slay Abel.

Jesus said, "You cannot *by taking thought* add a cubit to your stature." In other words, if you leave out God you cannot do much. There are psychological methods by which you can make the best of yourself. But when all is said and done, making the best of yourself is such a small step that it is hardly worthwhile. You will still be the same person. How much better to take the personality of today and change it for another thing. Instead of patching up the old, leaky boat, it is far better to scrap it and build a new ship. If you simply try to do your best with your own personality, it will beat you in the end. Cain will destroy Abel. Spiritual understanding lives only as long as you know that fundamentally you are Divine Spirit. Cleave to that and change your present self for something better.

So Cain kills his brother and Cain is left in possession. Man, having lost the spiritual idea, has forgotten that he had dominion over outer conditions. Man has held to the allness and power of materiality instead of the All-ness and Power of God. People, of course, have always professed religion, but to profess religion and to have religion are two very different things. If one considers the history of the world for the thousands of years that we know of, and particularly the centuries of so-called Christianity, and sees how people have behaved, then he will know how much religion they have had. The history of mankind has been a history of war, aggression, hatreds, and injustices. Why? Because Cain killed Abel and remained in possession. Man lost his spiritual dominion. If we had developed the spiritual faculty as rapidly as the intellectual faculty, then when all these great inventions came along, we would have used them for the betterment of people—improved living conditions, the destruction of poverty, and the abolition of class hatred.

Then we are told in this wonderful story that Cain was made a fugitive and a vagabond. He became a fugitive and a vagabond from the Truth of the Allness of God, which never came through again in any real fullness until Jesus did it at the expense of his tremendous consecration and demonstration. Mankind has been running about like a fugitive, looking for peace and freedom.

Everything has been tried by humanity, and as the centuries have rolled by it has tried them over and over again. In the Roman Empire they tried military organization. That failed and the Empire collapsed. Nevertheless, military conquest has been tried again and again. In the Middle Ages a theocracy was tried and that became so corrupt it fell to pieces too. In the eighteenth, nineteenth, and twentieth centuries it was hoped that natural science would set men free. On the contrary, we have used its discoveries for further destruction. Still more recently man has hoped that general education would abolish crime, hatred, and aggression. But Cain is still in possession.

In the Bible account, Cain becomes an outcast. Having slain Abel, he fears that the human race will wake up to the Truth and then he will be destroyed. When people find that the material belief ends in sin, sickness, and poverty, they will struggle against it. They will try to kill Cain, but because they are under the material belief, they will try to destroy trouble by using the trouble-limited mind, the intellect, which they at present possess. They will fight error with error, and that is going to mean still more trouble. All trouble is the brand of Cain. It is fighting error with error. When we are sick, sad, worried, or depressed, we have the brand of Cain upon us.

Now, the account says, "Whosoever slayeth Cain, vengeance shall be taken on him sevenfold. And the Lord set a mark upon Cain, lest any finding him should kill him." We get nowhere by saying, "I will have nothing to do with this material world. I will forget about the intellect. I will just sit and pray." We need the intellect for the things of everyday life: buying, selling, conducting business, building bridges and houses and airplanes. But the intellect will not take us into the things of the Spirit, and we should not allow it to restrict the knowledge and understanding of higher things. Cain is not to be slain. He is to be recognized and brought into the balance of mind and heart.

So the account goes on to say that Cain went out from the presence of the Lord and he dwelt in the land of Nod, on the east of Eden. The land of Nod means the dream that we are all dreaming of being under the dominion of all the disagreeable things that come into life. But the Bible gives hope, for it places the land of Nod to the east of Eden. The east always stands for the sunrise, for hope, for spiritual regeneration. Wherever the Bible shows us some of the unpleasant things that can come into our life, it adds the promise that mankind is going to overcome them. So even Cain, when he dwells in the land of Nod, which is east of Eden, is going to be redeemed.

Humanity is going to be free. That time will come, and I believe sooner than some of the most optimistic people think. We are not always going to dream this dream of danger and fear and hatred and distrust and conquest and aggression.

The blood of Abel cries from the ground to be resurrected, and in that resurrection, Abel, the keeper of sheep, will have a new demonstration. The lingering half-beliefs in mind over matter will have given way to the knowledge and power of spiritual thought control. Abel will no longer let himself be swayed by the arguments of the intellect, for he will know that his true power lies in keeping his thoughts centered on God, and Christ within.

Abel was the first shepherd in the Bible, and then there is a long procession of shepherds, culminating in Jesus, the Good Shepherd. Each of these shepherds adds something to the diagrams for living as the human soul makes its way through the corridors of time.

With the advent of Moses, the human race had come a long way. More and more of the educated people, usually the priests, were beginning to understand the power of thought. Moses was one of the most learned men mentioned in the Bible. He had been educated for the Egyptian priesthood, which meant he had the best education available in those times. Yet he had to become a shepherd before he did his great work of leading the Israelites out of captivity. Thus does the Bible emphasize the importance of getting one's thoughts right before undertaking any important work.

Although Moses had been brought up among the most learned men among the Egyptians and undoubtedly had access to the royal court, he had Hebrew blood in his veins. At that time the Hebrews were in bondage in Egypt, being the slave people. Thus it was that when Moses saw an Egyptian mistreating one of the Hebrews, he interfered and killed the Egyptian and buried the body in the sand. So he fled from the jurisdiction of Pharaoh, the King of Egypt, out into the desert, where he had an experience that led to a complete change in his life.

Several young women had come to a well to draw water. Some shepherds came along, and, also seeking water, they drove the girls away. Moses was quick to interfere in behalf of the young women. To show their appreciation they invited him to accompany them home, and told their father, the priest of Midian, what had happened. The priest was not one of an organized church, for there was no such thing in that part of the country. He was just a wise and spiritual man. In that Eastern desert country, hospitality to strangers was a virtue, and the priest asked Moses to stay with them. Eventually Moses not only was adopted by the priest but he married one of the daughters. Then, as the son-in-law, he went out and tended the sheep. Thus it happened that Moses was one of the great shepherds in the Bible.

It was while tending sheep that Moses witnessed the burning bush at Mt. Horeb. It was there that he got his illumination. This is highly significant. His illumination came while tending sheep; not when he was being educated in all the learning of the Egyptians; not when he was trying to run other people and knocking them on the head if they did not do what he told them. It was when he minded his own business and went out in the desert alone to *clear his thought* of upsetting things—getting money, position, honors, etc.—that he got his illumination.

So Moses was a shepherd, and we are told in this remarkable text, the last two verses of chapter 46 of Genesis, that the Egyptians could not tolerate a shepherd. Egypt in the Bible stands for trouble and limitations of all kinds, especially physical matter, e.g., the belief that your body has dominion over you, and can act up and give you all kinds of ailments. The Egyptians hated a shepherd, one who keeps his thoughts, and so the Israelites had to pretend they dealt in cattle. In other words, if you are the good shepherd, the "Egyptians" hate you because you are going to conquer. Pharaoh, King of Egypt, is your lower self that forgets thought control and prevents you from getting on faster than you do.

Jesus says, "He that entereth not by the door . . . but climbeth up some other way, the same is a thief and robber." If you try to demonstrate something that you are not entitled to by right of consciousness, you are a thief and a robber, and you cannot keep it. People in all walks of life try to demonstrate that for which they do not have the consciousness and then wonder why things do not work out for them. They have not been the good shepherd. They have not kept their thoughts right. Even many respectable churchgoers are really trying to get certain conditions of life without supplying the necessary mental equivalent. Many people try to get friends without radiating love. Many are trying to demonstrate wealth with a poverty consciousness, or with the desire to cheat or get the better of their fellow man. Others want a healthy body, but they have not even obtained some degree of peace of mind. As Jesus said, if you try to climb up some other way, you are a thief and a robber, and only trouble will come that way. He is emphasizing again the need for strict control of one's thoughts if one is to achieve that which he really desires.

Jesus follows up this idea by saying, "I am the door of the sheep; by me if any man enter in he shall be saved." The Jesus Christ teaching is the gateway to salvation, not in some distant heaven but in the immediate now. The "door" or "gate" is another very important Bible symbol. Passing through a door or a gate signifies a change in consciousness. When you pass from one room to another, or from one field to another, symbolically you pass from one state of mind to another. "Gate" or "door" means understanding and it also signifies dominion or power. In the Bible we so often find two different meanings or two aspects of the same thing. In this case the two meanings are supplementary—understanding and dominion. Understanding gives dominion, and understanding comes with a change in consciousness.

So Jesus, the Good Shepherd, says, "I am the door," my teaching is the gateway to the new understanding, the uplifted consciousness, which leads to complete dominion. This promise of man's destiny comes to fulfillment in

Revelation 17:14. It says, "These shall make war with the Lamb, and the Lamb shall overcome them: for he is Lord of lords, and King of kings: and they that are with him are called, and chosen, and faithful."

The Book of Revelation is a very strange book in many ways. It has been much misunderstood, primarily because it contains some of the most complicated symbology to be found anywhere. You might ask, why, if God wanted His people to know something, was it not given straightforward without all these symbols. And the answer is that symbol is the universal language of all peoples in all ages. Symbology transcends language. Primitive tribes such as those that have disappeared from Easter Island in the Pacific have all used symbols. And it is because of these symbols that scholars have been able to understand the peoples of very remote times, and have been able to unlock ancient written languages.

Many religious groups have tried to use the Book of Revelation as a book of prophecy. Every once in awhile there is some sect that predicts the end of the world, and they usually base it on something they found in the Book of Revelation. However, the Book of Revelation is not intended to foretell what will happen to nations or peoples. It is a book of prophecy of what will happen to the individual soul. It is a book containing many diagrams for your personal living.

In this chapter 17 of Revelation, John lists some of the temptations and the seemingly insurmountable obstacles with which the soul is faced during its journey through life. All are portrayed in symbol, and, in one of its rare instances, the Bible puts the whole reference in capital letters to emphasize the importance of the message. It says, "MYSTERY, BABYLON THE GREAT, THE MOTHER OF HARLOTS AND ABOMINATIONS OF THE

EARTH." And it says this was written on the forehead of the scarlet woman.

To the people for whom this was originally intended, Babylon had a special meaning. Babylon was the place where the Israelites had been in captivity for years. Their homeland, Judea, had been invaded, their cities destroyed, and they were carted off to Babylon. This was the second captivity. The first had been in Egypt, which stands for bondage. Egypt means matter, giving power to material things. It is the belief that your body is susceptible to disease and decay and that you have to put up with it. It is the belief that your security depends upon your job, your stocks or bonds, your insurance, etc., and that you are at the mercy of every economic ill wind that blows. That is Egypt, obvious, definite.

The Babylonian captivity came much later, and the Babylonian civilization was a great advance upon Egypt in many ways. Babylon was the New York and Paris of the ancient days. It was the center of fashion and culture. It had wide avenues and great buildings and one of the seven wonders of the ancient world, the so-called Hanging Gardens of Babylon.

Babylon meant prosperity for many of the captives, but as so often happens with great prosperity, many of the Israelites forgot God completely. As in every great city, there were temptations in Babylon. They worshiped many heathen gods. They relied upon astrologers and soothsayers. They indulged in all kinds of heathen practices, and little by little the one and only true God was forgotten. These are the subtle things that destroy the soul. Babylon is more subtle than Egypt. That is why the reference begins with the word MYSTERY.

Babylon stands for negative attitudes, not just the belief in materiality as represented by Egypt, but the belief in certain states of mind. For example, accepting low spirits, depression, and fear, instead of making your peace with God and getting free of Babylon. Accepting a sense of guilt instead of clearing it up and liberating yourself with God's help; allowing criticism, resentment, jealousy, and condemnation of others to stay in your heart—this is Babylon. As you see, these are more subtle things, and the subtle things are always harder to deal with. They creep upon us often without our hardly being aware of them. We come to accept them as a way of life.

So Babylon represents the belief, admitted or not, that we must have these negative states of mind; that we must go through periods of depression and fear; that we must put up with our feelings of inadequacy; and there is nothing we can do about them.

John speaks of the scarlet woman of Babylon. Woman always stands for the soul; and scarlet always represents the emotional nature—and in this case, the emotional nature in its negative aspects. The scarlet woman takes on many guises. For example, it is the state of mind where you let your emotions have free rein and run away with your common sense. It is the state of mind where you say, "I am going to have fun now; I can catch up with God later." It is the state of mind where you say, "Well, evil isn't real, so I can do this thing I know I shouldn't do, but I can get away with it." Or even if you think evil is real in a philosophical sense, you say, "I can be dishonest and deceitful, because God is good and kind, and when I have gotten what I want, He will forgive me." It is also the state of mind that believes everything it hears or reads, puts the worst construction on it, gives in to fear, and then decides there is nothing it can do because conditions are too strong for it. These are all various forms of the scarlet woman; and as you can see, you are not being the good shepherd, for you are not keeping your thoughts right.

And then John speaks of the beast with the seven heads and ten horns. These seven heads represent the Seven Main Aspects of God,* or rather the neglect of them. In our present stage of spiritual development we can know God in seven different ways, and as we understand them more, we develop spiritually. Everyone has a better understanding of some of these seven aspects than of others. For example, some people understand God as life and they demonstrate good health. Others understand God as love, and they get on well with people, etc.

The spiritual life, of course, is not so cut-and-dried as that. The important point is that as we understand more deeply the meaning of these seven aspects, the more easily will we demonstrate over our problems. When we neglect to develop them, this beast with the seven heads causes difficulties.

The ten horns represent our executive power. We have ten fingers, which represent the same thing, as does the decimal system that we use. The ten horns are the old Oriental symbol of power and are used to emphasize the fact that we have the power to use our spiritual assets constructively and creatively or destructively and detrimentally.

And then John gives the prophecy that not only will the individual come to know the Truth, but the Truth will spread over the world. Babylon will be destroyed. Symbolically, fire and brimstone and burning is the cleansing action of spirit; and all the nations and peoples standing and saying, "Here is the great Babylon! How powerful it was! How subtle it was in deceiving the nations of the

---

* See "The Seven Main Aspects of God" in *Alter Your Life*.

world; but it is gone"—all of this is prophetic of the erad-
ication of fear and all its concomitant evils, and the es-
tablishment of worldwide peace and prosperity. As the
individual hearts are cleansed, so will the hearts of the nations. The worst things in the individual, our fears, our
doubts, our unforgiveness, our holding to grudges and
jealousies, will pass away. And these things will pass away
from the nations too, and wars and rumors of wars shall
be made to cease, and the wolf and the lamb shall lie
down together and none shall be afraid.

Now, if we had to overcome these things by ourselves,
who could do it? But the Bible tells us that lined up
against all these subtle difficulties and temptations is the
Lamb of God. When Jesus got his illumination, John the
Baptist looked and said, "Behold the Lamb of God." He
did not mean that Jesus was the only person who could
reach God in that way. It is the wish and intention of God
that we should all reach it in fullness. But Jesus had done
it. He became the Good Shepherd, the Teacher, the
Wayshower. The Lamb means the spiritual idea, the spiritual Truth, and this account says that these negative
things "shall make war with the Lamb, and the Lamb
shall overcome them: for he is Lord of lords, and King of
kings: and they that are with him are called, and chosen,
and faithful."

Who are the called? Every one of us. God is no re-
specter of persons. We are all called. He has no favorites.
He sends His rain on the just and the unjust. He loves
the sinner as much as the saint, but He wants him to become a saint for his own sake.

The chosen are those who choose God. All the great
ones of history who have used the spiritual approach,
both those inside the Bible and outside, were chosen of

God because they chose God by really turning to Him in faith, day in and day out.

And the faithful are those who trust in the Truth. It is not just a question of being faithful in the day of triumph. Are we faithful in the day of trial? Are we faithful when we are discouraged and fearful, when the lower things in us and outer conditions seem to conspire to hold us back? If we hold on to the Truth, in the face of these things, then are we really faithful.

For a little time, it may seem that the negative things make war against the Lamb of God. For a little while these things may frighten and confuse us and try to discourage us, but as we become first the shepherd who keeps his thoughts right, then the good shepherd who lets his love go out to bless his fellow man, we will find that the spiritual idea will triumph over Babylon. The Lamb of God shall overcome the negative beliefs and states of mind, for he is Lord of lords and King of kings. The good shepherd is transformed into the Lamb of God, which has complete dominion.

CHAPTER 7

The Fourth Man

Then Nebuchadnezzar spake, and said, Blessed be the
God of Shadrach, Meshach, and Abednego, who hath sent
his angel, and delivered his servants that trusted in him.

DANIEL 3:28

T HE account of Nebuchadnezzar and the fiery
furnace is one of the most remarkable and dramatic examples of the power of prayer in the
Bible. It is another one of the stories that most people
know, but if one were reading it for the first time he
would find it full of surprises. Because people are familiar with these Bible stories, there is a tendency to take
them for granted—like the Empire State Building or the
Eiffel Tower.

I believe the story is true historically. We have no reason to doubt that these three young men who occupied
a prominent position in Babylon did excite the jealousy
of the authorities who perhaps saw their own power wan-
ing. The one thing some people cannot forgive is another's success, especially success that they do not have
themselves.

74

These three young men had ability, and they were promoted to a position corresponding to the governor of a state in the United States. They were appointed because of their ability and understanding, which was obviously due to the fact that they worshiped the one true God, whereas the Babylonians worshiped any number of gods. They had more than we have today. There was an idol of some kind on practically every street corner and people worshiped them. We have many idols too. We do not call them that. We call them position, knowing the right person, having an "in," "money talks," etc., as we run about from one thing to another to get ourselves out of trouble or into something "good."

The three young men, Shadrach, Meshach, and Abednego, worshiped one God, and when things went wrong, they did not run from one thing to another. They contacted the one God in themselves and were able to be of great use in Babylon. They followed the principle that Jesus later taught. They stayed right where they were and demonstrated there. They did not run away from their problems. Of course, one can never really run away from his problems, although many people try to. Our problems are in our consciousness and we take that with us wherever we go. So we find our problems waiting for us when we arrive.

In this story we are taken back to the old Oriental world. In those days Babylon was a great metropolis, much ahead of its time. As we have already noted, there were wide avenues and tallish buildings. There were the great hanging gardens, one of the seven wonders of the ancient world. There were shrines and markets. There was a steady stream of caravan traffic, and river barges laden with fruits and spices and other precious commodities. And there were pagan rites, and ecclesiastical and political corruption. The only thing missing was a modern airport!

King Nebuchadnezzar had sent out a decree, and everyone was gathered in Babylon—the princes, the governors, the captains, the judges, the treasurers, the counselors, the sheriffs, and all of the rulers of the provinces. It said, "At what time ye hear the sound of the cornet, flute, harp, sackbut, psaltery, dulcimer, and all kinds of music, ye fall down and worship the golden image that Nebuchadnezzar the king hath set up."

Long before this the Jews had been taken captive and brought into Babylon, and they had entered into the civic and cultural life of the land. A great many had fallen away from their religion, but there were others who had clung to the knowledge of the one and only true God. So on this gala occasion, there were these three Hebrew officials who jeopardized their high positions by refusing to bow down to the golden image. They had much to lose in a material way, and disobedience to a king's command in those days meant death.

Shadrach, Meshach, and Abednego had found the one true God. They had the one thing in life that really matters. So when Nebuchadnezzar commanded them to bow down to the image or be thrown into the fiery furnace, they answered, "Our God . . . will deliver us out of thine hand; O king. But if not, be it known unto thee, O king, that we will not serve thy gods, nor worship the golden image which thou hast set up."

They were ready to stand up for what they believed. It was a demonstration of real faith. We all have faith when we do not have to face a serious condition, but the real test is when we are right up against the problem. If we had the faith of these three young men today, there is no reason why anybody "thrown into the fire" would not come out all right. We demonstrate over small things, but when the big thing comes along we put our limitation (our limited belief) on God, and we suffer from that limitation. We may have faith that a broken leg or a cut finger can be healed, but we do not believe we can restore an arm. We think if we are thrown into a river and pray, God will get us out . . . or we will swim. But when it comes to our "fiery furnaces," we do not think God can save us. But please note that the limitation is not on God's part but in our own belief.

In the Bible, every story about people who lived thousands of years ago is a story for you and me today because the Bible is the Book of Every man. If I had my way, I would have all Bibles published with this phrase printed in large letters on the outside cover: THIS MEANS ME. And I would have covers in "jazz" colors. For a starter I suggest red, white, and blue. So many young people are frightened off from the Bible. Black is so somber and forbidding!

Well, this story of the three young men in Babylon means you and it means me. These men had great faith in their God. They had really found Him and that meant they were ready to stand up against any condition. They knew God and that was sufficient for them.

St. Augustine once wrote, "Thou hast made us for Thyself, and our hearts are restless until they find repose in Thee." That is the story of man, the great search of mankind, the end and all of living—to find God. Man searches for all kinds of things, not knowing that his search is really to find God, for in finding God, he has found everything. Natural science is coming to that conclusion. The more science delves into the mysteries of the cosmos and the more it discovers of the physical universe, the more it realizes that in the end, the whole scheme of things will only be explained in metaphysical terms.

This is really the search of mankind, to get closer to the Truth, to find God at last, and our hearts are restless until they repose in Him. Man does not always know this, but it is really what he is seeking; just as every raindrop, although it does not know it, is really seeking the level of the great sea, and will ripple and splash, and twist and turn, and bubble and boil, until at last it makes its reunion with the sea.

Men and women run over the face of the earth looking for security, trying to be safe, trying to get rid of fear. They seek it in money, position, force, cunning, and sometimes in drink or drugs. But there is no sanctuary except in Divine Love. In this great Bible story we are told in very dramatic form of three just men who had found that sanctuary. They put God first and would let nothing come between them and God. They had completely overcome fear by knowing God. Indeed, this is the only real antidote for fear.

Many books have been written and lectures given purporting to save us from fear. We are given little psychological tricks to play upon ourselves, a kind of sleight-on-mind, so that fear will go—but it never does. People go to psychoanalysts and psychiatrists to get rid of fears and phobias, and very often these same professional men are suffering from their own fears and do not know how to get rid of them. Many ways have been tried to eradicate fear. All have failed, because there is only one remedy: find God and know Him.

Sometimes people get rid of fear temporarily by pushing it down into the subconscious. Psychology calls this repression. But in the end this only makes matters worse. It is like trying to cure a rash on your hand by hiding it with a glove. There is only one way of eradicating fear, and these three men, Shadrach, Meshach, and Abednego, had found it. They relied completely on God. When you have God in your heart, nothing on the outside really matters. No more breaking your heart for things that do not really matter; no more destroying your health with ambition or caring what other people think; fear has gone.

Continuing with the story—Nebuchadnezzar had the young men bound hand and foot and thrown into the furnace. It was no ordinary furnace, as the Bible emphasizes, for the heat was so great that it slew the guards that got too near. And then something very strange happened, strange and beautiful. The king looked into the furnace and to his astonishment he saw the three men walking around, completely free, and even more amazing, *he saw a fourth man.* Although Nebuchadnezzar had been an idolator all his life, he realized the fourth man looked like the Son of God.

So, on that strange day, the Presence was dramatized, and the king saw it . . . and great changes followed. Up to then Nebuchadnezzar had thought that the only way to impress people was to frighten them, to keep them under subjection. Now his outlook was completely changed. He was convinced. Perhaps he did not fully understand, but at least he believed. He stopped religious persecution and made it possible for the knowledge of the true God to be taught to the people.

It has happened before and it has happened since that when people have been in grave danger or tribulation, strange help has come to them and things have changed, sometimes very dramatically and in a way they hardly dare think about. They sense a Presence, not with the eyes of the flesh, but they are aware of it, and it is like unto the Son of God.

There are infinite depths in every chapter of the Bible, and the deeper one goes, the more one finds. Going below the surface to what we would call in these days the psychology of it, we see that Shadrach, Meshach, and Abednego stand for the same thing as the three horsemen on the Black, Red, and Dun horses in the Book of Revelation. They also stand for the three sons of Noah. In other words, they stand for your physical body, your feeling nature, and your intellect. It is *they* who live in Babylon; it is *they* who are in the fire for the time being. Remember, Babylon means limitation just as Egypt does, but Egypt means more especially physical limitation—poverty, pain, ill health; whereas Babylon means mental limitation—fear, self-reproach, willpower, etc.

Now, mankind has reached the stage where we have gotten out of Egypt, or at least we know there is a way out if we are willing to pay the price in prayer and right thinking. But we are still in bondage in Babylon. We are in bondage to Nebuchadnezzar who can keep us in fear and worry and frustration, and yet he really has no power against those who realize the Presence of God and serve Him. If you fall down on your knees and worship the golden image of the king of Babylon by giving way to your fears and frustrations, you are the bond slave who serves him. If the three young men had bowed down when they heard Nebuchadnezzar's band coming along the street, they would not have been thrown into the fire. However, they would have been thrown out of their places as governors and would have been slaves for the rest of their lives. Having stood fast to the Truth, they came out of the furnace to govern Babylon, and they saw to it that the king reigned in honor and decency as well.

Whenever anyone finds himself in the fiery furnace, if he holds to the Truth against what may seem to be insurmountable odds, he will see a fourth man. This is the spiritual self. This is Pneuma, God in man. It is the fiery furnace, as a rule, that brings out the son of God within us. If, as soon as you are thrown into the fiery furnace, you turn to God with the full weight of your being—then the fourth man will appear—your true self, the God in you.

The Jesus Christ teaching comes to the world to show us that these three young men, these three parts of our being, are subsidiary to the fourth young man who is the Divine Presence in ourselves. We have to demonstrate through the other three but we must not allow them to be the governing power. Shadrach means "zealous in this matter," and represents the feeling nature. Meshach means "Where is God?" It is the body that asks "Where is God?" when it is in pain and agony. Abednego means "the servant of light" and represents the intellect. When these three move together and are balanced, the fourth man emerges—the spiritual presence.

Another important symbol used in connection with this idea in the ancient world is the sphinx. The sphinx has the body of an animal and the head of a man, and on the forehead is a little serpent or adder. The animal represents the physical body, and the man's face and forehead stand for the feelings and intellect, the personality or psyche. The little adder stands for the spirit, and if we go a little more deeply into it we will see why spiritual power in us comes like an adder.

When you are living in contentment with material things, completely satisfied with yourself, you are Nebuchadnezzar, king of Babylon. One starlit night Nebuchadnezzar went up to the roof of his palace. Stretching out on every side was the magnificent city of Babylon. As he proudly surveyed the splendor that lay all around, he exclaimed, "Isn't this great? And I built it! *Me!*" Well, that serpent stung him and he was brought down to "eat grass"; brought to ruin by the serpent, because nothing but suffering would bring him to himself. The power of God does sometimes come in the form of an adder.

So the sphinx represents the fourfold nature of man, but in the ancient world these truths were kept from the people. What we are presenting in this book was known only in the ranks of the priesthood and under the most appalling secrecy. Not until Jesus did his work on Calvary was a great change brought about in the race mind that made it possible for the people to get the full Truth. Before that it was the purpose of organized religion to usurp the power of the people and rob them spiritually, but today nothing can prevent the truth of the Allness and Availability of God from going out to all the people.

In the secret orders of the ancient world, one of the most important secrets was the riddle of the sphinx, and in this connection there is an amusing story told about Alexander the Great. When he visited the Temple at Heliopolis he sent for the dean and said, "Now, about the riddle of the sphinx, I want to know about that." This put the high priest in a difficult position. If he refused to tell Alexander he would be tortured abominably. At the same time, if he broke his oath and gave away the secret, he not only would be tortured by his own people but equally important, he would suffer, or so he thought, on the astral plane as well.

The high priest shrewdly answered, "We don't usually tell people these things, but you are Alexander the Great and that makes a lot of difference." Of course, Alexander was flattered that his importance was recognized. He leaned back and said, "All right, let's have it." The high priest then said, "What is it that walks on four legs in the morning, two legs at midday, and three legs at night?"

Of course, the obvious answer was "Man." Alexander was perfectly satisfied with the explanation: as an infant man crawls on all fours, as a man he stands erect and walks on two legs, while in later life he needs the aid of a walking stick.

However, there is a much deeper meaning to the riddle of the sphinx that was well concealed by the priesthood. In the beginning mankind believes in four things, namely, body, feeling, intellect, and spirit; but he thinks all four are equally powerful. Then the time arrives—midday—when man becomes more rationalistic and believes in only two things, feeling and intellect. But finally, after he attains spiritual illumination, he has all three phases—soma, psyche, and pneuma, as the Bible teaches.

It is recorded that in later years Alexander wept because he could find no more worlds to conquer. The great tragedy of his life is the tragedy of man through the ages; he had not learned the riddle of the sphinx; he had not discovered the spirit in him; he had not found *the fourth man.*

CHAPTER 8

A Tale of Two Women

And she had a sister called Mary, which also sat at Jesus' feet, and heard his word. But Martha was cumbered about much serving, and came to him, and said, Lord, dost thou not care that my sister hath left me to serve alone? bid her therefore that she help me. And Jesus answered and said unto her, Martha, Martha, thou art careful and troubled about many things: but one thing is needful: and Mary hath chosen that good part, which shall not be taken away from her.

LUKE 10:39–42

S O much has been written about the teaching of Jesus and the healings that he performed and the wonderful things he did, that we are apt to forget that like many of us, Jesus had his burdens to bear. Thus at times he found it very comforting to sit down with his personal friends, just as we do, and have a meal and a friendly chat.

In this 10th chapter of Luke, we have an interesting account of one of the beautiful incidents in the life of Jesus. He was with his friends, Martha and Mary, people whom he loved and with whom he could relax and have fun. Does that word "fun" shock you? I am sure that Jesus was full of fun, the kind of fun that made one glad to be with him. Man is the only "animal" that can laugh, and if God had not intended that man should enjoy himself, he would never have given him that power.

Of course, one's religion should be taken seriously but only in the sense of being earnest, not in the sense of being sad or grave. God never intended that we should go around looking like a rainy day. The Bible says, "The joy of the Lord is your strength," and Jesus himself constantly reiterated that he was full of joy and that he wanted his joy to be in us. Undoubtedly he had a keen sense of humor.

On that particular day he was there with Mary and Martha, and they were getting the meal ready—or at least Martha was. She was bustling around, doing all the necessary things, while Mary sat quietly at the feet of Jesus. And we know what happened. Martha chided Jesus for not making Mary help with the preparations. I suspect that most women in their hearts, and a good many men too, have had a sneaking sympathy with Martha. They have said, "Well, after all, Martha was doing all the hard work. Mary should have been helping too."

However, that is really to misinterpret the story. Jesus did not mean that you could neglect your duties and throw them onto other people. And we cannot excuse this by saying, "Well, I believe in God. I am just going to pray." Jesus did not mean that at all. Obviously that would open the door to laziness and hypocrisy.

These two women symbolize two different aspects of the human soul. They represent two different phases of human expression. Jesus understood that, and of course he knew the capabilities and the mentalities of his two friends. Most of us who have close friends see their failings and their shortcomings, and we see their good points too, and we love them all the more because we understand their natures.

So Mary and Martha represent two different phases of expression of the human soul. The Martha expression, going about and getting things done, is necessary until one has reached the Mary consciousness. This does not mean the avoidance of work, although Martha thought so. The really spiritual person will do whatever is necessary. And Jesus was no exception. One morning he built a fire on the shores of the lake and had fish broiling over hot coals, because he knew Peter and the others would come ashore damp and hungry without having caught a thing. At another time, he washed his disciples' feet.

In this Bible story, the Mary consciousness is not the avoidance of work. It is not the seeking of an easier path. It is the attainment of the higher path where one prepares the way for the greater demonstration. If Martha had but known it, her work was much easier and everything went better because of Mary's prayers. By engaging with Jesus in the deep things of Spirit, Mary was helping to lift the burden that Martha could not have done herself. That is why Jesus said, "Martha, Martha, thou art careful and troubled about many things: but one thing is needful: and Mary hath chosen that good part, which shall not be taken away from her."

It often happens with a husband and wife, or two sisters, or a sister and brother, that one is more spiritually advanced than the other. This makes it easier for both to demonstrate. Mary had reached the point, as Jesus knew, where she was under the Christ principle, and Martha was not. She did not have this consciousness just because she was sitting with Jesus. She was sitting there because of her spiritual development. If Martha had thrown down the dishes and said, "All right, I will sit down and pray too—it is less tiring," she would still be Martha and would not have the consciousness that Mary had.

Mary was under the Christ law, and when you are under the Christ law, the world is different for you. What do I mean by the Christ law? I mean understanding the spiritual idea, knowing that true prayer, which means some degree of realization of God, does more practical work in the world than all the material activities.

This story of Mary and Martha is historically true. Jesus did know these two women and their brother Lazarus, and he did spend that evening in their home. But like all the accounts in the Bible, it is also a parable, with a lesson in living.

This story teaches that it is prayer with some realization of God that matters. This is represented by the Mary consciousness, the Mary activity. It is not just saying, "I am going to repeat the Lord's Prayer" or "I am going to pray." That is fine. Of course you must do that, but that is not the Mary consciousness.

The Mary consciousness as expressed in the story is the state of mind where you know, with some realization, that God is the only Presence and the only Power. When you can do that, things happen, and the burden begins to lift. It is not that you are leaving material activities to be inactive, but rather that you are leaving a comparatively weak activity for a more powerful one. This is not an easy thing to do. It means preparation and practice to produce the consciousness.

If you have never had a music lesson, you cannot sit down at the piano and merely say, "I am going to play like Paderewski," and actually do it. If you want to play as the master plays, you will have to do what he did. First build up the gift by long hours of practice. Or, to take another example, it is a nice warm summer's day and the lake looks fine. You cannot plunge in and swim if you have never learned how.

So you cannot say, "I am going to have the Mary consciousness," and expect to have it. And you cannot just say, "I am going to put myself under the Christ law because that means happiness and peace." Of course it does, but first you must prepare the way by practice and discipline.

Mary had reached that point but Martha had not. Although Martha was a splendid soul or she would not have been a friend of Jesus, she did not have the higher knowledge or the understanding that spiritual consciousness changes the material world much more than mere outer activities without prayer. Martha did not have that spiritual consciousness. So the proper thing to do was what she was doing.

We have to demonstrate where we are. If you have the higher consciousness you will use it, naturally, but if you have not, you must do the nearest and the necessary things. It is a delusion to imagine that you can say, "I will let the work go . . . Instead I will read the Bible . . . It is much easier than washing the dishes, or mowing the lawn, or bathing the baby." You do not have the consciousness just because you say you do.

Mary had gotten where she was because she had taken the time and had developed through discipline. She had persevered in practice until she had reached the Christ consciousness.

Prayer will do anything and bring about any good if we can get high enough in consciousness. Until we do, we must do what we can. We must demonstrate on the level where we are. We must be doing our level best, and our level best is the highest we know at any particular stage of development.

We shall never rise in consciousness if we neglect the prosaic duties of daily life. Unless we do our day's work in the factory or the office or the field to the best of our ability, we will not get higher in consciousness. If a father is not a good father to his children; if a husband is not a good husband to his wife; if a son or daughter is not a good child to his parents; he cannot hope to rise in consciousness. One cannot expect spiritual growth unless and until he is doing his duty.

The first duty is to start where you are and fulfill your responsibilities in the best way you know. If you are a policeman in the street, a magistrate on the bench, the governor in the capital, you must fill that office as a public trust as honestly as you can—if you want the higher consciousness. In short, there is no substitute for the spiritual growth that comes from doing one's daily duties. We must meet our family responsibilities, our business duties, and our obligation to the community if we want to grow in spiritual power.

So Mary was not just taking it easy and listening to Jesus talking in order to get out of helping her sister in the kitchen. That is not what happened at all. Martha thought so, but Martha did not have the spiritual understanding.

Every person must demonstrate at his own level. If you are high enough in consciousness to demonstrate over a physical challenge without resorting to material or medical aid, fine, but then you should see the "health spring forth speedily." That is the test. How do you know if you are ready to do without a doctor? Easy. You will get well when you treat. If you do not get well, then have a doctor. If you are sick, give yourself a prayer treatment. Remind yourself that you are divine spirit. Claim the Presence of God. If you can do this effectively the sickness will disappear. If it does not, then you must do the next best thing.

It is a superstition to think that to take material steps will keep you back. The modern metaphysical movement has been going on for over a hundred years, and it has been thoroughly tested. I do not know how many people have died prematurely and would be alive today if they had taken reasonable material steps. They tried to do it by prayer and they were not ready. If one tries to do it by prayer and is not ready, it is willpower, and willpower is like taking a violin in one's hands and saying, "I will play like Heifetz." We have to demonstrate where we are.

There is a story about two ministers who were crossing one of the Scottish lakes. This was in the days before roads and automobiles. A person got to his destination by getting into a boat and being ferried across the lake. These lakes are sometimes treacherous. Storms come up suddenly. A boat can be capsized and people drowned within five minutes on what had been a beautiful and calm day.

These two ministers wanted to cross the lake. One was a tall, husky, six-foot country man with muscles like a blacksmith, and the other was a small, weedy, studious townsman—the long and the short of it. They hired a boat and the old boatman got out the oars and they started off. In about five minutes' time a terrible storm came up and churned up the lake. The boat was rocking and the boatman said, "Me lads, you'll have to help me. Grab hold of those other oars if you expect to come out of this alive." So the two clergymen picked up the oars and began to bend their backs. It was pretty hard work, but for a few minutes they kept the boat straight into the eye of the wind. Suddenly the storm got worse. The husky minister threw down his oars and said, "Let us pray." But the boatman yelled, "No, no, the little 'un can pray, but you keep on rowing."

This is what we are talking about. If one could get high enough in consciousness, he would speak the Word and the storm would subside. That is what happened on the Sea of Galilee when Jesus saved the disciples in a severe storm. The disciples said to one another, "What manner of man is this, that even the wind and the sea obey him." Jesus had the consciousness. The Scotsmen did not and so they had to take the necessary material steps.

There isn't anything that prayer won't do, but it must be prayer. You must seek God and seek Him whole-heartedly. If you are putting only part of your reliance on God, you will demonstrate accordingly. It is whole-hearted prayer that is answered. It is not the prayer of the learned; it is not the prayer of the sanctimonious; it is not the prayer of the powerful that is answered. It is the prayer of the wholehearted that gets results.

Mary had this consciousness. She probably did some re-markable things. Undoubtedly her prayers would help Jesus with the raising of Lazarus from the dead. She did not have Jesus' understanding, but she must have been a person very high in consciousness. Consequently, she could afford to sit at Jesus' feet, not neglecting her ma-terial duties, but rather the better to fulfill them by prayer.

So this is the tale of two women who represent two facets of the human soul. Each was serving God at her own level of understanding. Each was expressing and demonstrating in accordance with her consciousness.

In like manner each one of us demonstrates where we are, and if we want to express something higher, then we must provide the higher consciousness to correspond. We do that, not by grumbling at the conditions we find around us, but by living up to the highest we know, and by continuing to lift our consciousness by our daily prayers and meditations.

CHAPTER 9

War in Heaven

I N chapter 12 of the Book of Revelation we have one of the greatest diagrams of the destiny of the human soul. It begins, "And there appeared a great wonder in heaven; a woman clothed with the sun, and the moon under her feet, and upon her head a crown of twelve stars."

The Book of Revelation, often referred to as the Apocalypse because it is a prophetic revelation of the human soul and its destiny, is perhaps the most extraordinary document ever written. When you have the key to the Apocalypse, other achievements of the human race shrink in comparison, because it deals with the total thing—the nature of man, and the plan and self-expression of God.

The Apocalypse is a drama, but not the kind of play that belongs to our Western tradition. It was written by John under the instruction of Jesus Christ. It says, "the Revelation of Jesus Christ, which God gave unto him . . . ; and he sent and signified it by his angel [spirit] unto his servant John: who bare record of the word of God, and of the testimony of Jesus Christ, and of all things that he saw." Jesus made the revelation to John on the island of Patmos.

All through the Book of Revelation, John portrays, with the use of the most complicated symbology to be found anywhere, what happens to the human soul both individually and collectively. And here in chapter 12 we have the women clothed with the sun. This is the way God sees the human soul, and it is a preview of what you are going to be when you have realized your union with God, just as all the saints and mystics have done. They may have approached it from different angles but they saw the same vision.

John says, "There appeared a great wonder in heaven." From our limited point of view is it not a wonder that it could happen at all? When one thinks of how much fear man has experienced all through history and how many difficulties and problems he has faced, this state of mind is indeed a greater wonder. But the "woman clothed with the sun" is promised in such a way that we know it can be done. It is not just a counsel of perfection or a great ideal that is inspiring but out of reach. It is within our reach as a vision of things to come, a diagram of our ultimate destiny.

The "great wonder" means that at last the soul will realize its oneness with God in a way that cannot be put into direct language. Old things will have passed away. Nothing will have the power to terrorize you or take away your faith in God.

The "woman clothed with the sun" means that you are clothed with the presence of God. In nearly all of us the divine spark is sleeping: there is fire but it is only smoldering. "The moon under her feet" is the symbol of conquest. To have your feet on a thing means that you have subdued it with understanding. The moon always means the subconscious mind. Thus, the soul has become mistress of the subconscious. She is not at the beck and call of every thought that drifts in from the race mind. She is not easily frightened, nor is she readily diverted by self-doubts. "The moon is under her feet"—the subconscious mind has come under her control. She now knows that the subconscious can be redeemed, and that all the old repressions and negative accumulations are being eliminated. And so about her head is a crown of twelve stars.

The number twelve means all-round completeness. The twelve stars of the crown symbolize the twelve signs of the Zodiac, which represent the twelve different facets of the human character. Each of us has one predominant facet to be developed in each incarnation, but the soul that has completely found itself has the whole twelve. That does not mean that one has had to reach absolute perfection. You may say, "I do not feel I am becoming a woman clothed with the sun. I am full of faults and misgivings." However, if you are really on the spiritual path and striving toward the spiritual goal, you are on the way to becoming the woman clothed with the sun.

The Bible explains it in this manner: "She being with child cried, travailing in birth, and pained to be delivered." Jesus made the statement that when a woman is in labor she has sorrow because her hour is come, but as soon as she is delivered of the child, she remembers no more the anguish for joy that a man is born into the world. The woman clothed with the sun has not achieved perfection yet. She has seen it but has not realized it. The Wonder Child is striving to be born, and of course it is the soul that gives it birth. The soul is the mother, but the new child is your new self, born from the body of your old self. Although she is clothed with the sun and the moon is under her feet, yet the child is not born. That represents all of us on the spiritual path. The labor is almost over and the child is about to be delivered. All accomplishment involves effort, but when we are on the spiritual path it should be a joyous effort in expectation of the good to come.

The Revelator then sees another sign: a great red dragon. He has seven heads and ten horns and seven diadems. He stands before the woman, waiting for her to be delivered so that he may devour the child.

I think we know that dragon only too well. The Bible gives us the key. It is a red dragon, another aspect of the red horse.* The color red in the Bible always stands for the emotional nature. The thing that lengthens the labor and tries to kill the child is the emotional nature. It is the lower aspect of the emotional nature—physical sensuality and the love of the outside world. With some people it is the physical dominion of the body that hampers spiritual progress. With others it is love of money, power, domination over others. Always it is with uncontrolled emotion. The red dragon waits. He has seven heads and ten horns.

In occult literature the horn is always a sign of power. Ten horns means tremendous power. The red dragon of emotion for a time rides high; he has the power of manifestation or expression. The seven heads means that it seems as though he were everywhere, hydra-headed. It is the emotional nature that grips us and holds us back from unity with God and our fellow man, which torments us and wrecks our body. The seven heads of the dragon represent the opposite, or the ignorance of the Seven Main Aspects of God. The seven heads epitomize the seven principal temptations we are likely to meet: lust, greed, hatred, jealousy, vanity, false pride, and misuse of power. For a time the dragon is pleased with himself. He

_____
* See "The Four Horsemen of the Apocalypse" in *Alter Your Life*.

has a crown on each head. Of course, they are false crowns.

The child is to be born who will "rule all nations with a rod of iron." And the "child was caught up unto God." And the woman fled into the wilderness where a place was prepared for her to be nourished for "a thousand two hundred and threescore days." The number is not to be taken literally. It simply indicates an indefinite time with fulfillment at the end of the period.

Those who are on the spiritual path know the power of God. They know there is no power in matter or time or space but they have yet to prove it; so they are in the wilderness. When their first glimpse of oneness with God faded out, it was not lost. It was caught up to God to be preserved for them.

So we start demonstrating our "new thought." It is not easy. Anyone who says that following the higher path is easy has never tried it. It is not easy to conquer ourselves, to choose the higher and not the lower, to be truthful and honest and loving and pure and wise. It may appear easy on paper, but it is very difficult in the office, the home, and the street—difficult, but not impossible.

There is war in heaven. Michael and his angels go forth to war with the dragon. And the dragon and his angels fight, and the dragon, the deceiver of the whole world, is cast down to earth. He is cast down by Michael, the leader of the angels. Michael is the Bible term for re- minding yourself that these terrors have no power over you. When you remind yourself that sickness and mis- fortune have no power over you, then Michael is with you. Michael fights the dragon, and fear begins to dissolve.

In metaphysics we call this the *denial*. We deny that there is any power in matter. We deny that the appearance is real. We deny that the thing or condition, whatever it is, can harm or hurt us. We do not deny that a sick man is sick on the physical plane, but we deny that his condition has any power over him, and consequently he *can* overcome it. That is scientific denial. We do not deny the body, but we deny that the body has the power to make us sick or cause pain or trouble. That denial is the angel Michael, who goes forth to war with the dragon.

Now the war in heaven is going on within everyone who is earnestly and sincerely upon the spiritual path, for this dragon of the emotional nature is in every corner of one's life. As you drive it out of one place, you will find it in another. But the angel Michael fights on. As you keep on denying the power of the dragon, he is eventually "thrown down to hell," which is a dramatic and picturesque way of saying that the emotional nature is completely controlled and conquered, and at your command.

So, back to the first verse, you are the woman clothed with the sun when you believe this. No matter how unworthy you may be or how little you think you know about these things, if you believe in your oneness with God and give no power to conditions of the body or things of the world, you are the woman clothed with the sun. The moon is under your feet, and upon your head is a crown of twelve stars. You have the thing now. You have but to realize it. That will be the work of days, or weeks, or years. But the time of unfoldment does not matter because now you are convinced that Truth is true. Someday you will express everything that is potentially a part of your character. The twelve stars of the Zodiac will be as a crown around you, meaning that you have understood, assimilated, and are now expressing everything God means you to be. It is much easier to do it in this Apocalyptic age than it has been for nineteen centuries.

CHAPTER 10

Miracles

And the children of Israel said unto [Moses and Aaron],
"Would to God we had died by the hand of the Lord in the
land of Egypt, when we sat by the flesh pots, and when
we did eat bread to the full.

EXODUS 16:3

THE idea of the miracle runs all through the Bible; yet this is an idea that the modern world has largely lost. From earliest times right down to the Middle Ages, people believed in the miracle. During the Renaissance and later in the industrial revolution the idea of the miracle was almost completely blotted out in the increase in materialism and the consequent decline in spiritual perception and demonstration. However, in this New Age that we have entered there is an increasing awareness of the miracle and the power invested in man to bring dramatic changes in his life and circumstances.

The Bible teaches the miracle from Moses to Jesus. Biblical students who do not believe in miracles have missed the whole point. They are overlooking the very

99

dominion that God has given them, for the Bible teaches the omnipresence of God, and the dominion of man. God did not give dominion to a blind law, or to circumstances, or to so-called cosmic arrangements. Rather, he gave man dominion over himself and all things. If one does not catch this point, he fails to understand the Bible or the true teachings of Jesus.

We are divine no matter how many mistakes we have made. If we have been walking in the wrong direction, we can change. That is the idea. We have freedom of will and that involves dominion; because if we have the power to go wrong, we also have the power to go right. That is dominion, and dominion often involves a miracle.

What does the miracle mean? It means that having called upon God, things will be different from what they would have been had we not done so. It means that no matter what the difficulty, the power of God can overcome it. It means that no matter what the mistake, it can be undone and wiped out.

The Bible is full of tall-minded thinkers, and Moses is one of them. From the time Moses obeyed his inner promptings when "he spoke with God" until he ended his days, he was a tall-minded thinker. In fact, Moses' tall-minded thinking produced miracle after miracle, even as Jesus did.

In Exodus 16 we find one of those incidents. Out in the wilderness, the Israelites were faced with imminent starvation, and Moses and Aaron and those with them who tuned in to spiritual power produced the miracle of the quail and manna. Hundreds of years later Jesus was to do a similar thing with the loaves and fishes. Exodus 16 tells us as plainly as language can that miracles do happen. In this case the quail and manna came out of the sky and provided food for the children of Israel.

Now, the laws of nature do not change, for one of the attributes of God is unchanging principle. What happened four thousand years ago could happen today in this modern world if the necessity arose, and if anybody had the understanding and scientific faith of Moses, Aaron, and Miriam. Sometimes it seems as if the miracle violates law, as with Jesus walking on the water. We call such things miracles because we cannot explain them by any of the known laws. There is a great deal of psychic phenomena that cannot be explained because we do not yet know the laws governing such things. But in the sense of breaking the laws of nature, there are no miracles.

The Bible shows us that what we generally see as the laws of nature is only a small part, or cross-section, of the laws. As we learn more and more of the powers of our minds we will do more and more extraordinary things. There have been some advanced souls like Moses and Elijah and Jesus who have understood these powers and demonstrated them because they had their minds tuned in to the higher spiritual levels.

So there are indeed miracles in the sense that extraordinary things happen that seem to defy the laws of nature, and they have happened thousands and thousands of times. The fact that the quail and the manna came out of the sky, or were precipitated out of the circumambient ether, only points up the truth that there is nothing impossible to tall-minded thinkers when the need arises.

Read the account of Moses carefully and you will see that God never did anything directly but always *through* Moses. Moses would commune with God. He would get his inspiration to do a certain thing, and then the needed thing would take place. The whole story of Moses and the Children of Israel exposes ordinary human nature to the full light of day. It shows how a few individuals, Moses and Aaron and Miriam, could surmount all kinds of incredible obstacles and do extraordinary things by making their daily contact with God.

The Children of Israel had an experience similar to the early colonists in America. Having escaped from tyranny, they were beset with all kinds of problems in the wilderness of the new land. Even as the man without a job has more freedom but also some new problems, so the Israelites no longer had to toil without pay making bricks without straw. They were free, but now they had to fend for themselves.

One would think that the Israelites would have rejoiced with gratitude over their newfound freedom. However, to anyone who has dealt with a cross-section of human nature, it should come as no great surprise that the Israelites had only been out of slavery a month and a half when they began to find fault with Moses and what seemed to them a situation even worse than before. "When we were in Egypt we were slaves, yes, but we knew where tomorrow's dinner was coming from. We did not have to look around for food and shelter. We sat around the fleshpots and we did eat bread to the full. Here we are in the wilderness and there is no one to give us food."

The experiences of the Children of Israel are figurative of what happens to everyone who is really on the spiritual path. The Children of Israel symbolize anyone who really believes in God and the power of prayer. A mere academic belief in God is of little use. Millions of people say they believe in God, but they do not believe God is particularly interested in them. If you take this attitude then you are not an Israelite in the Bible sense and you can expect no miracles. But if you say, "I believe in the power of God . . . I believe He is interested in me and that I can contact that Power to comfort me, heal me, enlighten me, purify me . . . I believe God is working through me to solve this seemingly insoluble problem"—then your mind is in tune with the Infinite. You are beginning to do some tall-minded thinking. That means the time has come for you to remember the power of the miracle. It means the time has come for a great thing to come into your life.

Jesus said we could move mountains and so we can. He did not mean material mountains. That would only be a conjuring trick. He meant mountains of difficulty and trouble, mountains of fear and frustration and doubt. He said we could do it if we had sufficient faith in God. There is no limit on the side of God, but we put a limit on our faith and understanding. That is why some people can demonstrate over some things and others cannot. In practice, the only limit on demonstration is, "How well is your mind tuned into God? How tall are you thinking?"

The only difference between Moses and his followers was in the quality of their thinking. Moses thought tall. He got higher in consciousness. His followers groveled down at the level of the problem, and on that basis they would never have been saved. It was only through their higher spiritual selves, symbolized in the story by Moses, that they could get themselves out of difficulty. So long as we wrestle with the problem, we get nowhere. We are trapped in a circular cage and the only way out is through the top.

Every grief or difficulty means the time has come to go a step higher. A problem is not a barrier. It is a challenge. It is important to take the attitude that your spiritual promotion has presented itself in the guise of a problem or difficulty, and you are to take another step forward. And this calls for effort. If you want to go higher, you must climb the steps.

In Paris, up in the Montmartre, a place of fun, art, and gaiety, there stands the beautiful, shining white church of the Sacre Coeur. From almost everywhere in Paris it can be seen standing as a shining white sentinel both day and night. To get up to the Sacre Coeur you wind through endless narrow streets, up, up, up, with many blind alleys and dead-end streets. Finally, you turn a corner and there stretching up to the Sacre Coeur are dozens of gleaming white steps. It has been a long climb and you are tempted to say, "Oh, I don't want to climb anymore." But then you would miss the best of all. On the other hand, if you say, "Well, I've come this far," and you climb those steps, you experience one of the unforgettable sights of the world. Lying at your feet is the whole of Paris—the River Seine winding like a silver thread, the Eiffel Tower piercing the sky, and the tomb of Napoleon and Notre Dame and many other well-known buildings—all bathed in the golden light of a summer's afternoon.

And so it is with life. If you want to go higher, you must climb the steps. If you think, "This step is too high, I can't take it," it is your choice. If you think, "This trouble is too much. It is so unfair"—then you stay below until you wake up to the knowledge that you can do it. However, if you meet each challenge with the realization, "God in me is stronger than anything I have to meet. God has given me dominion over my circumstances. I let nothing in this situation frighten me for I know God is with me," and continue in that vein, you will get your further spiritual understanding, and you are on your way to your miracle. It may take time and prayerful effort, but you will get it, just as the Israelites did.

Now these were not highly spiritual people—what we might call saints. If they had been they would mean little to us. They were like us, some good and some less than good. There were murmurings among the people. Typical of human nature, they forgot the demonstrations they had made, the flight from Egyptian bondage and the parting of the Red Sea. And they forgot the suffering and oppression of the slavery from which they had escaped. Faced with starvation in the wilderness, they looked back with nostalgia and cried, "Why did we ever leave Egypt?" But in their heart of hearts they knew they were free and freedom is something worth having.

The Bible says, "The Lord spake unto Moses." That was Moses' higher consciousness, his divine contact, that spoke to him, as it does to everyone who listens with an open mind. Moses came to the point where he knew that spiritually he could demonstrate over the problem. The Bible mentions that Aaron and Miriam helped him, and undoubtedly there were others whose consciousness was sufficiently high to assist in the demonstration.

How did they do it? How did they produce the miracle? Did they sit down and picture loaves of bread and fat cattle? Did they try to conjure up food in some way? No, of course not. Every miracle is produced by a realization of the omnipresence of God, by knowing there is no place where God is not. They harmonized their consciousness with the universal law of omnipresent good. They put themselves in tune with the Infinite. They realized the presence of God. In other words, they made God and His abundance real to themselves. Nothing can happen to you except that which is real to you in the depths of your heart. So they had to make the presence of God real to themselves. They realized their basic unity with God and that God cannot leave man, His own expression, without the things he needs. They reminded themselves that peace and harmony and right action are part of divine providence.

Then the miracle happened. The food they needed made its appearance. The quail came and the manna came, a new kind of sustenance that they had not known before. God always opens new ways and new means for the mind that is in tune with Him. God is always ready to produce a miracle for the tall-minded thinker. Fundamentally, tall-minded thinking means the uplifted consciousness that rises above the level of lack and knows that the power to solve the problem or create the new thing is coming from God, and that there is no limit to what God can do.

Jesus summed up the miracle technique by saying, "What things soever ye desire, when ye pray, believe that ye receive them, and ye shall have them." In other words, in every miracle there is the great element of faith that what is needed, God has already provided. It is not a question of making something happen, but rather uncovering the good that already exists in the Mind of God. That is why, for example, in the feeding of the five thousand, Jesus knew that he could continue dividing the loaves and fishes so long as he gave thanks in faith for what he did not see with the eye of the flesh. It was this clear perception of the Truth of Being that made it possible for him to heal the impotent, the lame, and the blind. While these things existed as a matter of fact, they had no existence as a matter of Truth. Others, including those directly involved, saw the difficulty. Jesus saw the perfect man, the perfect thing.

Tall-minded thinking does not grapple with the problem. It is a quiet knowing that you are the instrument of Divine Power. Such a mind can speak the Word and get a full-dress miracle if need be.

CHAPTER 11

Can the Stars Help You?

They fought from heaven; the stars in their courses fought against Sisera.

JUDGES 5:20

C HAPTERS 4 and 5 of the Book of Judges combine to tell one of the most remarkable stories in the whole Bible, and they form one of the outstanding pieces of literature in the world. Chapter 4 tells the story, and chapter 5 is a wonderful primitive poem romanticizing the story. It was originally recited as a kind of duet, with dancing, tambourines, and singing—a dramatic expression of a great incident in the history of the Israelitish people. It lifts us right out of the twentieth century, back almost before written history, and gives us a glimpse into the ancient past.

This Book of Judges is a strange and even horrible book, until you have the spiritual key. Like the Book of Joshua it is full of bloodshed, and of human beings, real people. Indeed, most of the people in the Bible are real people. They are the counterparts of people we know. We have

107

been their neighbors, have gone to school with them, have made friends with them, have quarreled with them.

In depicting its characters, the Bible does not try to make them look better than they were. It gives them to us as they were because it is not afraid of the Truth. When you find a book, a newspaper, an institution, a leader, who is afraid of the truth—beware! The Bible tells us the worst about Moses as well as the good. Other chapters tell us the bad as well as the good about David, about Paul, and about Jacob. It does not gloss anything over.

So, in this chapter of Judges, it tells us what went on in those days. We see these primitive, barbarous people as they were, fighting their way into this new land and battling with the heathen nations around them. There were twelve tribes, and they were not even at peace among themselves. They quarreled vigorously, and only the menace of the heathen around them kept them together at all.

The Israelites had gone into this land together, and during a period of some three hundred years there was no regular selected leader. The word "Judge" in this case really means a leader—a leader of guerrilla warfare. He was not a judge on the bench, as we would use the term. The tribes were moving around, fighting for their lives. They had no capital city, for it was long before they had gotten Jerusalem. Later, under David, they were woven into one people with a strong central government. But at the time they were disorganized and facing complete subjugation by the heathen.

And God raised up a leader! As He raised Abraham Lincoln from the backwoods cabin, and George Washington from a cultured and wealthy eastern home, so at that particular time He raised up Deborah. She led her people against what seemed to be insurmountable odds, and came out victorious. There have been only a few women in all the long history of the human race who have done that kind of thing. The old Empress of China was one, and comparatively recently in the Western world, there was Joan of Arc.

Deborah was what we might call a natural leader. She got tired of seeing her people robbed and murdered by the surrounding heathen, and she decided to do something about it. She looked around for a suitable general, and she found him in Barak. And she told him what to do. Deborah, with her personality and her spiritual understanding, took the reins and the people were saved. The Bible calls her a prophetess, which means she was turning to God for inspiration and guidance.

The twelve tribes of Israel would not interest us today if we read them as a matter of history. Their importance to us lies in the fact that they stand for the foundation faculties of the human soul, and the lesson here is that unless all your faculties are oriented toward one point, you are not going to conquer the heathen within yourself. You are not going to win freedom, health, and spiritual development. If you allow any of your faculties to take the easy way, you are not going to get the victory. But when Deborah comes along, she (the soul) unites these faculties in achieving the goal.

Some of the tribes were ready to fight; others were not. The writer says this tribe came out with a sword and that tribe came out with a sword, but the tribe of Reuben had talk around the water courses. That was the gossiping place in the East, the place where they sat around and talked. They were appeasers. They said, "Oh, the Philistines are not so bad. It will be all right." But if it had not been for Deborah, it would not have been all right. Deborah had taken her measures. She was a good strategist. She directed Barak what to do. And when Barak said he would only fight the battle if she were to go with him, she said she would. But she reminded him that in those circumstances it would not be for his honor, because Sisera, the opposing general, would be sold into the hands of a woman. There was a terrific battle and the Israelites won out against the Philistines.

There is another side to this story, which features another woman, a completely different type from Deborah. Her name is Jael. Sisera, the leader of the Philistines, was captain over nine hundred chariots and thousands of men. In those days the leader actually led the army into battle in hand-to-hand combat. Sisera and his army were chasing after the Hebrews who had been in retreat, but Barak under the guidance of Deborah turned the tide of battle. Most of Sisera's men were slain, and he himself had to jump out of his chariot and make a run for it.

He found himself going through an encampment of tents, out of breath and completely exhausted. Suddenly he spied a good-natured-looking woman in the doorway of one of the tents. She recognized Sisera but did not let it be known. Instead she said, "Come in. Fear not, my lord, I will take care of you." And she placed a mantle over him to seemingly hide him. This was Jael, the wife of Heber the Kenite.

So he lay down and asked for a drink of water, and she gave him some milk to drink. He felt he was extremely fortunate, but he was still a little apprehensive. He said to her, "Stand in the door of the tent, and if any one inquires of me, don't let them know I am here." She replied, "Trust me. You can go to sleep." And so the poor, simple-minded man . . . well, it is a tragic story.

As soon as he was asleep, Jael looked around for a weapon, and she found a long tent spike and a mallet. He was lying on his side, sleeping the sleep of exhaustion, and she took the mallet and drove the spike right through his temples, pinning him to the ground. That was the end of Sisera. As the Bible puts it, "At her feet he bowed . . . where he bowed, there he fell down dead." Presently her own people came along and she said, "I have killed the enemy," and they all rejoiced.

The Bible does not pretend that it is the right thing to do to invite a stranger into your tent and then knock him on the head. It simply records what happened and how Jael accomplished what she conceived to be in the best interest of her country. Today we would not work in quite that barbarous way, but I wonder if our more polite civilized way, the use of modern weapons, gives us the right to cast the first stone at Jael. At any rate it happened, and the story as a piece of literature is of extraordinary vivacity and dramatic power, coming into the twentieth century as fresh as the morning dew.

At the end of the story we are told something more about Sisera, which is full of pathos. He was the leader of the Philistines, a heathen and an enemy, but he was a man. According to his lights he was just as good as anyone else. He had a home where he was loved and a mother waiting for him. There was evidently a strong bond between this mother and son. When he went out to battle, his mother hoped he would come home safe and sound, as a mother would. But she also hoped, being of a barbaric people, that he would have killed a great many of the enemy and brought back a lot of the spoils of the battle. She was the queen mother of the tribe and had ladies-in-waiting. She was getting a bit anxious. She looked out a window and cried, "Why doesn't my son come home? Why tarry so long the wheels of his chariot?" She probably had an intuitive feeling that something was wrong. Before her ladies-in-waiting could give a reply, she answered her own question. "There has been a tremendous battle and they are dividing up the spoils. And he is going to get the best of the spoils; a damsel or two (the old harem idea), garments of divers colors." Her hobby was evidently needlework, and she added, "divers colors of needlework on both sides," the very best kind that could be done; and probably her thought was that he would bring this gift to his mother. But of course she did not know that at that moment he was lying dead in another woman's tent.

This epilogue about the home life of Sisera is a tragic touch and a very human one. We are apt to imagine that people different from us are not human, that they do not have feelings of gladness and sorrow, and all the things that make up life. However, the Bible does not forget all that.

The surface meaning of the story is clear. Those who choose God conquer and prosper. But behind that meaning is the symbolical or metaphysical significance. Every man and woman in the Bible stands for a state of mind. Deborah represents the state of mind where things have all gone wrong, but we are not going to sit down under it. We turn to God for inspiration and guidance. We know God is with us and so we get up and take our measures.

Sisera stands for the human intellect. In accordance with Bible symbolism, Sisera is slain through the temples because the forehead, the front part of the skull, stands for intellect. Every part of the body symbolizes some of our faculties. From the nose to the top of the forehead stands for the intellect, just as self-esteem has the back portion of the head.

Phrenology is a very misleading thing for most people because these things are *symbols*. It is almost universal that studious men and those who have used the intellect, do tend to walk with a slight stoop. And, of course, people with great self-esteem, who are exceedingly well pleased with themselves, walk with their heads tilted back. The weight of the back of the head pulls it back. These are more than mere fanciful things. The parts of the body do express our character.

Sisera stands for the person who relies solely upon his intellect, and the intellect has to be destroyed in the sense of being subordinated to the intuition and the other spiritual faculties. If you allow the intellect to rule, you will come to grief. This does not mean that the intellect is a bad thing. A good many people, particularly in the religious world, could do with a great deal more than they seem to have. The intellect is a fine thing, but you must be the master.

There is one more interesting facet to this story from Judges. The Bible text says, "They fought from heaven; the stars in their courses fought against Sisera." Is it true that the stars in their courses can fight against you? And is it true that the stars can fight for you? Is there such a thing as destiny?

Right up to the Renaissance everyone believed in astrology. The old Eastern civilizations, the Bible people, and Rome and Greece were very astrologically minded. You cannot understand the people of that day unless you know what they believed—and they all believed in something called destiny, in a rhythm in the course of the universe and the life of man. How far were they right?

For the last three or four hundred years, there has evolved the idea that man has free will to the point of omnipotence. My convictions have been molded under the influence of this spiritual evolution. I firmly believe that if you believe in God-in-you, you can go out and do wonderful things, amazing things, for your own good and the good of humanity. But there is such a thing as rhythm in life. Certain individuals and certain nations have a particular genius, and there are also certain things you cannot change.

Does any man suppose today that if he had been born a woman his life would not have been different? Does any woman suppose that if she had been born a man her whole life would not have been different? Of course it would, and these things you cannot change. You cannot change your type, but you can make that type perfect. You cannot be anything you like. Noah Webster did a great work but he could not have done Lincoln's work. Lincoln was a great man but he could not have done Edison's work. Each individual has a special faculty, a special aptitude, and his whole temperament, his nervous system, his intellect, all tend to that point. If you want to call that destiny, do so.

However, for practical purposes there is no limit to what you can do within the framework of your type. If you have a real desire that comes from God, you can fulfill that desire. There is no real desire without the potential ability to fulfill it, and there is no latent ability without the opportunities to call it into expression.

When the Bible says that the stars in their courses fought against Sisera, on the surface this means that Sisera's astrological chart was against him. As we have said, the people were very astrologically minded in those days. There is no question but that human beings are affected by times and tides and seasons and stars, or at least the ones we call planets. More and more, science is proving that everything in the universe is in beautiful balance. Everything has its influence on everything else. Shakespeare speaks of this. He says, "There is a tide in the affairs of men / which, taken at the flood, leads on to victory." And again, "It is not in our stars but in ourselves that we are underlings."

These two contradictory statements of Shakespeare are harmonized in the experience of Sisera. Being born under a certain sign of the Zodiac means that he came into the world with certain traits and faculties and characteristics predominant. It means that he was born with a certain psychological setup, and, apart from prayer, in any particular circumstance he would always react within the framework of that setup. And consequently he was bound to come to grief.

What do I mean by his psychological setup? I mean that Sisera thought along certain lines. He believed certain things. He had certain opinions and ways of living. He had certain fears. And that is true of each one of us. You have a certain psychological setup that makes you what you are. There is no fatalism about this, because you can change it. However, unless you change it, certain things must happen to you. If we want certain results in our lives, we have got to think and speak and act along the appropriate lines.

Sisera had thought and spoken and acted along certain lines that were bound to finish up in a great defeat and in his dying a violent death. He had believed certain things, held on to certain views, carried with him certain doubts and fears and weaknesses that could only lead to a particular end. That was the way he had thought and lived. Thus, "The stars in their courses fought against Sisera."

Sisera could have broken that chain of circumstances at any time, no matter what the stars foretold. Sisera could have changed his thought and turned to God, and the whole course of his life would have changed. However, Sisera was a Philistine and he did not know he could do that. His defeat was not in his stars but in himself.

The Philistines thought that certain wood and stone statues in their temples were gods. They worshiped different false gods, just as today so many of us worship idols. We worship microbes, germs, climate, depression belief, and the worst of all false gods, the calendar. Practically every home in the country has a calendar on the wall or on the desk, and every day good Christians kneel down and worship it. They say, "I am a day older," "The years are passing by," and "At my time of life." They are worshiping false gods. We laugh at the ancients because they had gods of stone and wood in their temples, but our false gods are all around us too.

Deborah, on the other hand, knew better than this. She saw that the odds, humanly speaking, were hopeless. But she did not think along these limited lines. She knew that there is a Power that is entirely good and ever available, and she went ahead banking on that.

Each person has his psychological setup that makes him what he is. There is no fatalism about it because if you do not like it, you can change it through prayer. At any time in your life, no matter where you may be, you can call upon the great Spiritual Force of the universe to come to your help, and it will meet your need if you let it. However, if you have made certain plans and if you insist upon following those plans, then God cannot act. You are relying upon intellect, and intellect can only take you along the accustomed path.

When you rely upon Spirit, as Deborah did, then everything is made new; the great odds against your success melt away. You will have the physical, mental, and moral strength to carry on. And you will live to see the day when you too can sing about your great victory over what seemed for a fleeting moment an insurmountable barrier.

CHAPTER 12

Marriage and Divorce

For this cause shall a man leave his father and mother, and shall be joined unto his wife, and they two shall be one flesh. This is a great mystery: but I speak concerning Christ and the church.

EPHESIANS 5:31, 32

M ARRIAGE is one of the most important, if not *the* most important, of all human relationships. It is a great training school of life. In America, nine people out of ten manage to get married—at least for a time. Thus it seems fitting that this question should be considered in our diagrams for living. Jesus thought marriage so important that his first public act was to attend a wedding. And Paul, in the fifth chapter of Ephesians, outlines some bold concepts out of which we can formulate a diagram for successful marriage.

There are some people who think marriage is as inconsequential as buying a pair of gloves; and there have been religious teachers who have taught that marriage is an evil thing, and that God is against it. Some people have pointed to the recently unearthed scrolls and the

117

Book of Thomas to prove that some of the early followers of the Christian message were against women and
therefore against marriage. That is a dangerous teaching that is usually founded on some psychological or psychic experience, and wherever it has been given forth,
it has ended in disaster.

However, normal people get married, or at least think
they will one of these days. Jesus, knowing that, and also
knowing that there were those who preached against
marriage, went out of his way to attend a wedding and give
his blessing to it. That was his first public act. Marriage is
a proper relationship and we must come to know the fac-
tors that make for its success.

Paul has many things to say on the subject of marriage.
His radical views on the duties of husbands and wives are
rejected as totally unrealistic by some, and are accepted
as a yardstick for marital behavior, "because the Bible
says so," by others. But for the most part people are confused and bewildered, and possessed of the uneasy feeling that somehow they are not living up to the Bible code.

It may be that Paul was just a crusty old bachelor; or he
may have had in mind specific instances among the people of Ephesus and some of the Macedonian cities; or
he may have been outlining a general moral code for
the times. However, as I have been saying, the Bible was
written for all people of all ages, and these accounts have
an esoteric meaning for those on the spiritual path. Thus,
when the Bible records these words of Paul, please remember that in this case "man" means the "I Am," the
conscious spiritual part of yourself. "Woman" or "wife"
means your soul; chiefly, in our modern terminology,
what is called the subconscious.

When we read ". . . let every one of you . . . love his wife
even as himself," it means that you have to develop your

human character and lift it more and more toward the divine. Where it says the wife must reverence her husband, it means you must learn to control the soul or the subjective conditions. Where it says "Christ and the church," that does not mean your particular church or somebody else's particular church. The "church" is your personality, which means you and your whole environment. So "Christ and the church" has reference to the extent to which you allow the Christ to be expressed in your life. The Bible is telling us—as it always does—that the individual must find God for himself and develop himself spiritually until he gets full and complete illumination.

Marriage is the most intimate bond in life. It is therefore important to remind ourselves that marriage is first of all a partnership, and any partnership should be maintained on a 50–50 basis. If marriage partners agree on the 50–50 idea, the marriage can hardly fail. On the other hand, if marriage becomes an 80–20, or a 90–10 proposition, something is bound to go wrong. Trouble in any partnership is usually caused by one partner trying to get more than he is entitled to. And so it is in marriage.

However, in marriage one person is often more spiritually developed than the other, and such being the case, the person who is more spiritually developed will have to be prepared to give more and take less. A partnership calls for some kind of sacrifice, and in marriage this is especially true.

Even mature people often expect their marriage to be one continuous honeymoon, but of course this is not the way life is. As a minister, it is frequently my privilege to perform marriages. It is really amazing how many people come to me in the expectation that I can open the book and hand them a happy marriage. Of course I remind them that the marriage ceremony is only the beginning, and the ultimate success of their marriage must be worked out by the individuals themselves.

There are certain things you must understand about yourself if you want to make your marriage a success. You must know that in practically every case the conscious mind of the man is positive to the conscious mind of the woman, and her conscious mind is negative to his. I am not using the word "negative" in a bad sense, but rather in the way that one might say the seventh step on the stairs is negative to the eighth step. On the other hand, the woman's subconscious mind is positive to the man's subconscious mind, and his subconscious is negative to hers. This is why a woman should use influence rather than direct force. The wife should, as far as possible, avoid *telling* the husband. Men do not like to be *told*. A woman can *indicate*—and God has given her a million ways for doing so. She can make her feelings known without telling him, and that is because her subconscious mind is positive to his. On the other hand, the man is inclined to use the direct approach because his conscious mind is positive to hers, and women need to understand this.

People imagine when they are getting married that they will live happily every after, but that is absurd. I speak as a hardened bachelor, but you know the onlookers see most of the game. And in my work of dealing with every kind of problem, I get to know a good deal about people. It is ridiculous to expect to live together month after month and year after year without disputes and difficulties arising.

When there is trouble in the marriage—and if there are no differences there is probably so much indifference that nothing matters—the more spiritually developed partner should get by himself and work spiritually until the anger is overcome. Never dare to open your mouth or take a step when you are angry. Get by yourself and dissolve the anger or resentment first, and then go straight to the partner and talk it out, rightly and clearly. Do not swallow things for the sake of peace, for if you do, they will fester in your subconscious and either come out in an explosion that will wreck the marriage or wrack the body. Ill health makes for difficulties in marriage because we are not our true selves unless we are healthy.

Second in importance in marriage is the simple thing of good manners. Good manners are the oil in the machinery of human relationships. Unfortunately, most people keep their best manners and their best behavior for strangers. Yet if you do not like your neighbor, you do not have to speak to him. If you do not like your business firm, you can change it. If you do not like a casual acquaintance, you can let him alone. But in the home, you cannot simply drop the members of the family—and thus good manners are called for. It is amazing that in many homes where knowledge and culture are taken for granted, good manners are often at a discount. The feeling is, "Oh, it's only my husband—or my wife."

Marriage cannot be taken for granted. It goes on indefinitely, and unless the relationship is taken care of, it will go to pieces. In other words, one must give some attention to maintenance. You spend a certain amount of money painting a house, replacing certain parts, taking care of shrubs and plants. You take care of your automobile. That is maintenance. In marriage, likewise, there needs to be an investment in maintenance, in upkeep, and it is surprising how careless an otherwise fine man or woman can be in considering the feelings of the only person who really matters to his or her happiness.

For instance, under no circumstances should you ever criticize your partner's family. If he wants to do it, let him; but don't you do it. Let him say anything he likes about his family, but don't you say it. The family link is made in infancy, long before he met you. He may have turned against his family, or he may have just awakened to the fact that his brother is a "very bad character." Still, in the inner layers of his subconscious there is an emotional link that will resent criticism from a nonmember of the family.

Where a couple have been married for some time, certain peculiarities will be observed in the partner. After all, each is a human being and everyone has certain idiosyncrasies and faults of character. In marriage it is only common sense to avoid treading on these sore spots. If the partner has a violent temper, avoid exciting him. Your own worst fault may not be temper but something just as difficult for you, so help him to control his temper and he will tend to help you to control your fault.

Suppose the other person has views that do not commend themselves to you? Why should you control the religion or the politics or the feelings of another? A true partnership stands on equal rights. So never try to control your husband's or your wife's religion, politics, or personal convictions. Giving him an opportunity for self-expression will tend to make his relations with you stronger, fresher, and newer. If you are a Democrat and your wife announces she is going to go out and help the Republican party, let her, as long as the rest of the marriage is smooth and she is taking care of her part of it.

Suppose your husband is suddenly bitten with the bug of astrology, and you, his wife, are infuriated. You ridicule his interest. You joke about the stars, and if anything goes wrong with him you say, "Aha! What about the stars now?" If he is satisfactory in other phases of his life with you, then let him have his occasional preoccupation with the planets and the signs. Whatever the hobby or the interest, do not ridicule it or you will undermine the relationship that exists. A hobby is only the outer symbol of something that is happening in the soul. That particular outlook is doing something for the person, and in opposing it you are really trying to destroy that inner thing. Leave it alone, and if it is sound, it will work itself out into the expression it needs. You must not be the one to explode it.

Each person in marriage is seeking in another the qualities that he feels he lacks in himself. This is the basis of sex attraction. Women look to men for strength and protection, for logic, and for the pioneering qualities they feel they lack in themselves. Men look to women for femininity, homemaking, motherliness, and receptive reactions, which in their own souls they seem to miss. This is why in general it is not wise for a woman to seem to be too clever especially before marriage. After marriage she can reveal her cleverness more, but men are a little afraid of women who seem to be too intellectual.

I am in favor of early marriages for most people, and I would urge present-day parents not to oppose young people in marrying. I believe that long engagements are not good. There is no guarantee that one will know the other more at the end of a long engagement than in a comparatively short period. A person will know more in the first month of marriage than in all the years that preceded it. Parents who have children of a marriageable age should not oppose marriage on the score of youth, nor because of finances. Young people should not expect to start life where their parents left off. Let them marry and attain the good position together.

The chief mistake that men make in marriage is that they rarely demonstrate their affections sufficiently. They take love too much for granted. They may say, "Oh, she knows I love her or I wouldn't have married her!" That is not good enough. Men seem preconditioned perhaps by early training to inhibit and repress their feelings of affection. Obviously this is out of place in marriage. It is not sufficient that a man should love his wife, for women are so created that they like to be told so, and need to be told so frequently.

A husband will find it very useful and important to make thoughtful gifts. He probably did it before his marriage, and there is no reason why he should not continue the practice. His gift should bear evidence that he has made a special effort of thoughtfulness of her. She knows the importance of symbols. It means a great deal to a woman to receive candy or flowers or other tokens of love at a time when there is *no* reason for it. And, of course, the husband should remember her birthday. A man usually tries to forget his birthday, and a woman pretends she wants to forget hers—but don't let the husband forget it! Also, he should remember their wedding anniversary, even if he has to arrange to have his secretary remind him.

I am certain that many men make the mistake of forgetting these things, even though they literally adore their wives. And I am just as sure that the wives have entertained considerable doubts about the marriage relationship because of this lack of tangible expression of affection.

And now to the women! Their chief mistake unquestionably is this: they allow the man to get the impression that he has sacrificed his personal freedom. It is not how things are but how you think they are, in marriage as elsewhere, that controls your life. Actually, a woman gives up as much freedom as a man does, but the man does not think so. Every man feels, sooner or later, that his personal freedom has been considerably abridged. Of course, if the marriage is a success, he feels he gets back more than he has sacrificed.

As a rule, men do have a more varied and diversified life, but whatever you do, Mrs. Wife, do not allow him to feel that all this has been cut off. Do not keep asking him where he is going. In a happy marriage he will not be going anywhere you do not approve of. Women should wake up to the fact that men have a standard of honor equal to their own. Most of the opinions to the contrary have been given by cheap novels and cynical plays that do not represent life. The majority of men have just as much self-respect and honor as women have.

But a man does not want to have to come home like a child to tell you where he was at three o'clock in the afternoon or with whom he had lunch. Eventually he will talk and it will come out, if you are tactful. Do not "clock" him in and out. That is all right for the factory but do not introduce it in your home. Do not let him feel that the whistle blows at six o'clock, or whatever time it is you expect him home.

Now, I am going to tell you something that you need to know, Mrs. Wife. Every married man needs to get away from women altogether now and again. If a man's mentality is to be kept balanced and wholesome, he needs now and again to get away with "the boys." He will come back to the atmosphere and sanctity of the home, strengthened and improved and inspired for having been away. It is a good thing for a man to be a man among men from time to time.

Marriage has an important karmic link. It is true that every relationship in life is a karmic link, but most of them are not so important. However, marriage is so important that if you run away from the problems of marriage, they will follow you until such time as you overcome them and put them right. There is not a bit of use running away from the difficulties of marriage because sooner or later you will meet these things somewhere, somehow, and you will have to solve them. What is the good of running from an unpleasant task at ten o'clock when you know very well you will have to come back and finish it at three o'clock? So in the training school of matrimony, people should recognize this and stand their ground and solve the problems if they possibly can.

BUT—and herein comes the question of divorce—there is a limit to what a man or a woman should be asked to put up with. When the thing is *absolutely hopeless* and the partner gives you no possible ground for making your marriage a success, then I think divorce is the best way out. There is no sense in prolonging the situation if it is, humanly speaking, entirely hopeless. However, if there is *any hope at all*, then stand your ground and work the marriage out with prayer. It is extraordinary the power that prayer has in making a marriage go right. Of course, if there are children involved, the problem is doubly serious.

Marriage is so difficult a school because it is such an intimate one. It covers every phase of your life, and you can never get away from it so long as the marriage exists. The tuition of the school is love. If you ever loved the man; if you ever loved the woman—that man or that woman is essentially the same person who stood with you through the ceremony. The original qualities are still there, and there is always a possibility of coming back to the original status—if you believe they are there and make an effort to relate to them and draw them forth.

I gave a course of lectures in London, at the end of which a woman approached me and said, "When I first came to these lectures six months ago, I was arranging with my lawyer to get a divorce. But I started praying, and now the man I was going to divorce has disappeared and the man I married has come back"—and turning around to him, she added, "And here he is." There are very few marriages that prayer will not redeem.

The question of marriage and divorce would not be complete without some mention of children and family relationships, for a great deal of misconception surrounds the idea of family duty. What is one's duty to his family? Divine Providence has so arranged it that we are all born and brought up in families; but one's family was never intended to be a bondage. One of the advantages of family life is that in the home one gets the truth about himself. The members of a family usually feel at liberty to speak to one another "straight from the shoulder." A brother and sister never feel any embarrassment in being frank with each other.

However, one must not allow his family to become a bondage to him; not that I want to break up families. No indeed! Although some families need to be broken up. And, thank God, in my short career I have broken up a few families—in the right way. I have persuaded brothers and sisters to stop living in the same house. I have persuaded grown-up children to move to a hotel or to the other side of town, even to another city. But that was to set them free and to set the parents free.

Certainly young children should accept guidance and parental authority; and older children should see that their parents should never want for necessities. However, the so-called "ties of duty" are sometimes overemphasized. Once a child reaches his late teens, he should never let his father or mother hold him back, mentally or spiritually. His parents were brought up a generation ago, but the plan of Providence is that each generation should do new and better things. Even if the parents do not recognize this, the children should.

Children must think for themselves. They must learn to choose their own politics, their own religion, their own friends, their own reactions to life. Of course they will make mistakes, but they will make even more mistakes by trying to remain in the old rut. A woman once came to me and said, "It's about my boy—he's getting into bad company." I asked her, "How old is he?" And she replied, "Forty-four." I said, "Well, I think it is about time he should!"

It is often much worse in the case of a girl who is brought up tied to her mother's apron strings. A boy is normally allowed more freedom. Sometimes there is that type of mother who just must have some creature to exercise her power over. She will not allow her daughter away from her side. She will not let her have any social life. She will not let her marry. Then in the course of time the mother dies, and the daughter by that time is middle-aged and deprived and insufficient mentally, physically, socially, and spiritually.

These are extreme cases but I wanted to make my subject very clear. Fortunately, these extreme cases are getting to be fewer every day. The old restrictions are breaking down. The mistaken authority is melting away. Indeed, the pendulum has begun to swing the other way in the breakdown in parental authority and a resulting "juvenile delinquency." While this of course is to be deplored, it is not so widespread as it seems. Millions of families are growing up together without the old strict family ties. Fine young men and women and emerging who, in freedom of choice and action, will be the leaders of tomorrow.

Parents must realize that children need love and guidance, and especially do they need parents and all that the word signifies. This is why divorce is so tragic where children are concerned. All children need the influence of balanced parents of a stable marriage to encourage self-expression and freedom, and to mold personal responsibility and self-reliance.

CHAPTER 13

What Jesus Taught About Christmas

> Behold, I bring you good tidings of great joy, which shall be to all people. For unto you is born this day in the city of David a Saviour, which is Christ the Lord. . . . Glory to God in the highest, and on earth peace, goodwill toward men.
>
> LUKE 2:10, 11, 14

THE problem connected with Christmas is the same today as it has been since the very first Christmas. Just what does it mean? Jesus came into the world. He did his work. He taught us and left us sufficient knowledge to find our salvation. And then he went away. Nineteen centuries later we have not yet found our salvation as a whole. And always it is the same reason— we do not understand the Christ message. We do not realize the true significance of Christmas or of Easter, nor do we comprehend what really happened on Good Friday.

We do not understand what Jesus came to do and why he did it. And it is this lack of understanding that keeps

130

us out of the kingdom of heaven. From the beginning until today Jesus has been the most misunderstood man in history. He was misunderstood by those who crucified him. He has been misunderstood by those who have hated him; and he has been misunderstood by those who have called upon or paid lip service to his name. Until we know something of what he came to do, what he really meant, it is not much use in calling ourselves Christians. Just calling upon his name means very little. He said more than once that just to say, "Lord, Lord," does not bring us into the kingdom of heaven.

Christmas is the most beautiful festival of the year. It is not coincidence that is the feast of the Wonder Child, the baby who grew up to change history, for Christmas symbolizes that mystical thing, the incarnation of God in man. With the advent of Jesus love was born into the world . . . and the thing called true humility. Those who had come before had taught justice, a God of grim mercy; but Jesus taught love and compassion. He put these things into the human race and they will never be uprooted.

Now, it is true that the Christian people have not always exhibited these things through the nineteen centuries since Jesus came. However, they are in the race mind now, and in the not-distant future the people of the world will begin to express them. We have stepped across the threshold into a new age, and these things will be brought into expression. The human race is going to cease to fear and hate one another. The time is coming and most of us will live to see it when these great truths that Jesus taught will be expressed all over the world.

To Jesus, divine love was the supreme and vital thing. No other human being has ever loved his fellow men as Jesus loved them. He was not sentimental about it. To him love was the keynote to life, the gateway to peace and harmony and right action. He loved mankind and he demonstrated it in his life and in his death.

The personal history of Jesus extends from the manger to the cross, about thirty-three years in all. The second chapter of Luke, which I think is the most beautiful chapter in the Bible, explains the birth of Jesus, that event that was to change the whole world. Luke is a great artist with words, and he tells the story with incomparable clarity and beauty. He was a highly cultured man, not a simple fisherman. Thus he had literary qualities that the other evangelists did not have. Luke was naturally a very kindly man. He was tolerant. He understood people. Professionally he was a physician—Paul calls him the beloved physician. Physicians are tolerant. They understand human nature. They make allowances. Sometimes the clergy are inclined to be too severe. They expect people to be perfect, but a doctor never does.

Luke begins by saying that there went out a decree from Caesar Augustus that the whole world should be taxed. This is actually a mistranslation. The Authorized Version of the Bible, the King James Version, is the best, but there are a few mistakes in it. The decree had nothing to do with taxation. What happened was that the Emperor decided to take a census.

We might ask ourselves at this point why Jesus came when he did. He was probably born 6 or 7 B.C. The modern calendar is based on the supposed date of birth of Jesus, but today we know that an error was made of six or seven years. But what does it matter? Why didn't he come generations before or after? The Israelites had been praying for a Messiah for hundreds of years. Why did he come at that particular time. The explanation is that that was the time for a great teacher because it was the first and only time that the world was one. Thus his message could be more easily taken all over the world.

However, we must remember that in those days the world meant the basin of the Mediterranean. Nobody knew anything about China or Japan or South Africa. The world for practical purposes extended from the north of Africa where the Sahara desert ends—up north to the Rhine and the Danube. North of those rivers the people were considered barbarians and nobody took any particular interest in them. And the world extended on the west to include Wales but not beyond. No one had ever heard of America, and on the east it went to the other end of the Mediterranean and a little bit beyond. That was the world, and in those days there was one emperor, one law, all over the world. It was the ideal time for the Savior to come.

Jesus' parents lived in the north of Palestine in the little village of Nazareth, but they were not descended from people there. They were from Judea, in the south, "of the family and lineage of David." Their ancestral home was Bethlehem, and following the law they went to Bethlehem in order to register for the census. Bethlehem means house of bread. As we have seen, a house symbolizes a part of your soul, your mentality. Bread in the Bible always means food; not just food for the body, but food for the soul—the food of knowledge, understanding, and spiritual experience. That is the food that God gives you. That is "the true bread from heaven." And Bethlehem, the house of bread, is the consciousness of that Presence.

The Bible calls it the city of David, and David means Divine Love, the Divine Love that dwells in your heart. A divine love outside of yourself, supposedly acting somewhere else, is about as much yours and has as much power to nourish you and keep you alive as if you put your blood in a jar on the shelf. Divine Love can only subsist for you in your soul. Nowhere else. You must experience it first-hand.

As Mary and Joseph approached Bethlehem, Mary was ready to be delivered of the baby. We are told that there was no room at the inn. The word "inn" in our Bible means a "khan." The khan was not an inn as we under-stand it, but an enclosure of four walls with a wide open-ing on one side. Khans were built and placed a day's journey apart on the roads from Jerusalem to Jericho, from Jerusalem to Damascus, etc. People used donkeys or camels, occasionally mules, and took their provisions with them. By going into the khan at night they had some protection from wild animals and possible robbers. And, of course, it was in the khan that one met other travelers and exchanged gossip and news with them.

On that occasion great crowds were on the road, and so when Mary and Joseph got to the khan, they found it full. This presented no great problem because there were a number of caves in the vicinity. Often these caves were used by shepherds and others for protection on cold or stormy nights, and they usually brought their animals in with them. This was the kind of cave in which Mary and Joseph spent that memorable evening. They had every-thing they needed. And there was a manger in the rock wall in which they could place the infant Jesus. The Bible calls it a stable, but there is nothing dreadful about that. In that old world people took better care of their ani-mals than they did of themselves. In any case, Mary and Joseph could have demonstrated anything they needed, but they were not looking for material things. The more people have of the spiritual, the less they need of the ma-terial.

As we review the Christmas story we must remember that everything in the Bible is allegorical as well as mystical. That is why in the Bible we find so many diagrams for living. Everything in the life of Jesus is allegorical as well as mystical. And of course, everything in our lives too is an allegory of our own souls. Everything that you do, everything that happens to you, is a dramatization of something in yourself. And the life of Jesus is a dramatization of the Christed soul, the soul that has chosen the spiritual path. So the life of Jesus furnishes many diagrams for living as we either follow in the Master's footsteps or try to go it alone.

When the Wonder Child arrived, he did not arrive in a royal palace as some thought he would, perhaps among the Herods. Many of the Israelites, who had been praying for the coming of the Messiah, thought that he would be born in a palace. They were expecting someone who would re-establish a material kingdom and restore the lost glories the Israelites had known under Solomon. And some of the more devout and holy people said he would surely be born in one of the ecclesiastical families attached to the temple; but he was not. He was born to a simple family, and in a stable.

The stable is symbolic of our present state of consciousness with its feelings of unworthiness. It symbolizes the Christ that is born into any one of us the moment that we give our whole hearts to God. That is when the Christ is born, when we make up our minds to put God first in our lives and not second. We feel unworthy, and that our heart is no place for the Christ. People mistakenly try to make themselves worthy. It is a waste of time. But if we turn to God and say, like the Centurion, "I know that I am not worthy that you should enter my house, but because you are Divine Love, in spite of all my faults and shortcomings, you can make me worthy that you should come to me," then the Christ does it. In other words, the Christ comes into a stable, not into a palace, but the Christ sanctifies and glorifies that stable so that it becomes the temple of the living God.

In the old tradition and the classical pictures of the advent, there are always a donkey, an ox, and a lamb in the stable, and these represent three aspects of our nature. The donkey represents this mind of ours that is often quite stubborn. The donkey has never been credited with very much intellect, wisely or unwisely. The donkey stands for the human mind unillumined by the Christ. The ox stands for the body, the pull of the animal forces that keep many people out of the kingdom. And the lamb represents our spiritual nature. The Christ is born and unites these three.

We observe Christmas in the last week in December. The early Christians wanted to woo their followers away from the pagan Roman celebrations. So they fixed Christmas to take the place of the Roman Saturnalia with its heathen practices. However, Jesus was not born in the winter. He was born in the spring or early summer. The shepherds, you will remember, were out in the hills with their sheep.

The shepherds of the Christmas story were simple people but very spiritual. For the last four hundred years since the Renaissance, the tendency in the West (in Europe and in America) has been to associate spirituality with culture and education. These go well together, but they are different things. In the Old World it was different. An uneducated man, a shepherd, a plowboy, a mariner, a fisherman, was just as likely as not to be a great saint—in the sense of one who is spiritual and has a contact with God.

And so these simple shepherds had a spiritual understanding. I did not say "poor" shepherds. How can a man
be poor who has all he needs? I do not suppose these
shepherds had anything but the clothes on their backs,
a simple hut to live in, and their sheep; but that was all
they needed. Yet they had something more. They had
the starry hosts above and the hills and the wind and the
ever-unfolding miracle of nature all around them. And . . .
they had time to think and meditate and gain spiritual understanding. They had a knowledge of God that hardly
any of the learned men of that day possessed, and they
knew that something important was happening. All the
clever fellows in Rome, Alexandria, Corinth, and other
places did not know a thing about it. But the shepherds
did. And the wonderful thing happened. An angel appeared.

Now in this day of great scientific achievement and
great materiality, there are some people who say, "The
appearance of an angel is a beautiful idea but of course
it could not happen. Perhaps the shepherds just imag-
ined it. It is not possible to see angels." And they are
right, too, as far as they are concerned. Only those who
have the angel vision will ever see angels. The angels are
the inspiration God sends in high moments of consciousness. God sends His angels in times of stress and
need and they bring an inspiring thought, a beautiful
idea. They bring healing energy. They bring joy. And
they tell you those lovely and ineffable things that you
never could know yourself.

Sometimes the angel Gabriel comes into your consciousness, and if you say yes to him, then something
wonderful happens. Something is born in your soul that
is with you for the rest of your life. But it is your privilege to say no, if you wish. When you are bitter or cynical,

when you give in to disappointment and resentment, when you are critical—these are only forms of the one negative activity—you are saying "no" to the angel, you are saying "no" to God, and consequently you are saying "no" to life. But I counsel you, I urge you most deeply, when the angel comes to you, say "yes." Do not make any excuse. Do not say that you can't believe it or that you are not good enough. Do you suppose God has any illusions about that? Say "yes" to the angel, and you are saying "yes" to the more abundant life.

When the angel first appeared to the shepherds their first reaction was fear. "They were so afraid." How human! How like us! They were frightened at first because it seemed too good to be true. This is the tragedy of human nature. We think something is too good to be true; but trouble never surprises us. We regret it, but we do not think it is too bad to be true.

When something new and strange happens the first thing that most people feel is fear. Most people tend to interpret anything unexpected as evil and danger. A great idea that has been helpful to many is "I see the angel of God in every change." Never be afraid because a change comes into your life. God never closes a door without opening another one. So when some change happens and you begin to be frightened, say to yourself, "I see the angel of God in this change."

So the angel said to the shepherds—and this is one of the most important texts in the Bible—"Fear not." A great prayer! "Fear not: for, behold, I bring you good tidings of great joy." And then there was a heavenly host of angels; because when the angel comes and you say "yes" to him, then you get far more than you ever dreamed. And the heavenly music broke out and they listened to it. And, again, those who hear heavenly music are those who have heavenly music in their hearts. There is always heavenly music going on, but it exists only for those who can hear it.

The angels brought the shepherds a message that they could understand. "For unto you is born this day in the city of David a Saviour, which is Christ the Lord. And this shall be a sign unto you; Ye shall find the babe wrapped in swaddling clothes, lying in a manger." Here was something they were familiar with—a manger. They probably knew the exact cave where the babe could be found. They had been told all they needed to know, perhaps as much as they could understand. How could anyone ever be told more? How could any of us be told any more than we are capable of understanding?

The Bible is full of knowledge and inspiration. The air is tingling with it, but the blind man cannot see the light, the deaf man cannot hear the music. And we are blind and we are deaf to the light of God and the music of the spheres. We do not see and we do not hear and we say, "It is not there," but it is. When Solomon became king of Israel, he did not ask God for riches and honors. He prayed for knowledge and wisdom and an understanding heart, and as a consequence riches and honors were given him in abundance.

These shepherds got their inspiration, they accepted the message, and they did not sit idly by waiting for something to happen. They went and found the Christ child. And of course, the one thing that matters in our lives from our birth to our death is for us to find the Christ child. We must find him for ourselves, find him in a stable and let him grow up and turn it into a palace, not a material palace, not one built with hands, the temple of the Holy Spirit.

Another important detail of the Christmas story is added by Matthew. Before he found the Christ in the person of Jesus, Matthew had been a tax gatherer. He sat at the receipt of custom, collecting duties from travelers and merchants who came through Jerusalem from all parts of the world. He had met many foreigners, and it was only natural that he would be particularly interested in some strangers who had come all the way from Persia to pay homage to the infant Jesus.

Matthew calls them Wise Men who came from the East. They were wise because they were spiritual. They had spent much time in prayer and living the spiritual life, and they knew that something wonderful was happening on the earth. They had seen a star and they followed the star and it led them to the babe in Bethlehem. People who keep near to God know many things that people who do not, cannot know.

The people of ancient times were very astrologically minded. We therefore find the Bible, beginning in the Book of Genesis, full of allusions to the twelve signs of the Zodiac. On the fourth day of creation, God said, "Let there be lights in the firmament of the heaven to divide the day from the night; and let them be for signs [zodiacal signs], and for seasons." In the Book of Judges, we find that the twelve tribes of Israel were arranged in camp according to the twelve signs of the Zodiac, and their banners depicted these signs. So it is not surprising to find that the Wise Men from the East were deeply interested in astrology, and that they followed a star to the manger where the Christ child lay. But what is surprising is that *there was not one star but two.*

For many years Bible scholars and students of religious history felt that this account of the star that the Wise Men followed must be purely figurative. But more recently some long forgotten documents came to light. Kepler, the astronomer and mathematician, had made some calculations back in 1603. In that year he observed a very unusual conjunction of the planets Jupiter and Saturn in the constellation Pisces. There was a heliacal rising of the two planets, which means they appeared so close together that they seemed to be one terrifically bright star. Following a hunch, he figured back from that year and found that 1,610 years before—the year 7 B.C. to be exact—the year Jesus was born—there had been a similar conjunction of the two planets.

So the star that the Wise Men undoubtedly followed, was actually Jupiter and Saturn in conjunction. And there is a bit of interesting symbology here because in the Jewish tradition Pisces was the zodiacal sign of Israel; Jupiter was considered the Royal Star governing the tribe of Judah; and Saturn was the Protector of Israel. Consequently, the Wise Men intuitively felt a great event was taking place in Judea. This was the star of revelation that rose in the east.

The star in the east is the morning star. It is the first gleam, the first dawning of the Christ Truth. In the Bible and elsewhere, as we have observed earlier, the east always stands for spirit, for truth. "The lightning cometh out of the east and shineth unto the west." When you see the star in the east you have not yet found the Christ child, but you are convinced that he exists and that you want him, and that you are going to find him. The Wise Men saw the star in the east and they followed it, and it brought them to the Christ child. They had been seeking God, and one always finds what he seeks.

After the child was born he was taken to the temple in accordance with the laws and the rules of the time. When you are trying to live the spiritual life you must meet the rules and regulations of ordinary life. You cannot be on the spiritual path unless you are a good citizen, a good parent, child, husband, wife, brother, or sister. So they took the child to the temple and there was the customary offering of two turtle doves that "all things might be fulfilled." The doves stand for inspiration. Later when Jesus began his public work with John the Baptist at the river, "the heavens were opened unto him, and he saw the Spirit of God descending like a dove, and lighting upon him."

At the temple, there was a saintly old man named Simeon who had devoted his life to God, and he too knew what was happening. It had been revealed to him by the Holy Ghost—divine inspiration—"that he should not see death, before he had seen the Lord's Christ." As we have said, when you give your full devotion to God you often learn things before they happen. Daniel knew what was going to happen to him. John the Baptist knew what was going to happen to him. Many others in the Bible have had precognition. And Jesus was the supreme example of this. So Simeon knew just what was happening, knew it months before, perhaps several years. And there was also a woman of great age in the temple, a prophetess named Anna. She too knew what was happening.

Both of these people gave thanks for the appearance at long last of the Messiah for which generations of people had been praying. When Simeon took the infant Jesus in his arms, he blessed God. Rather unusual. How often do we bless God? Usually we are too busy asking God's blessings on us to think of blessing Him. Yet blessing God is a powerful form of affirmative prayer, for it means sending thoughts of love and gratitude to the Giver of every good gift.

Simeon, having made his affirmation of love and faith, made this remarkable statement: "Mine eyes have seen thy salvation, which thou hast prepared before the face of all people [not just the Israelites]; a light to lighten the Gentiles, and the glory of thy people Israel." This was not a common concept at the time. Most people thought that when the Messiah came he would come to redeem and help only his own particular nation and race. But they were mistaken and Simeon knew it. Jesus came to redeem the whole of the human race.

"A light to lighten the Gentiles." This statement was prophetic, for when a Canaanite woman, a Gentile, came to Jesus to heal her daughter, his disciples tried to send her away. But Jesus said, "I am not sent but unto the lost sheep of the house of Israel." Turning to the woman, he tested her sincerity by saying, "It is not meet to take the children's bread, and to cast it to dogs." And she answered, "Truth, Lord: yet the dogs eat of the crumbs which fall from their masters' table." And so Jesus healed her daughter, remarking, "Great is thy faith: be it unto thee even as thou wilt."

Mary and Joseph having performed their religious duties went back to their home in Nazareth, "and the child grew, and waxed strong in spirit, filled with wisdom: and the grace of God was upon him." This is the beginning of the life of Jesus, beginning in the manger, and finally finishing on the cross.

Now, before Jesus came on earth he was a great spiritual being, and when he decided to come back on earth, he had to be born a human being. Was he God? Yes, and so are you. Jesus was God but not Infinite Spirit. The totality of God could not be limited in a human form. Jesus was the expression of God, the individualization of God, just as each one of us is. However, Jesus knew he was God, and we only hope and vaguely believe we are, but we do not know. When we know, then we shall be able to do the works that Jesus did, as he promised we should.

What did Jesus think of Christmas? What did he think of his birth on earth? I am sure most of us have asked ourselves the same question about ourselves. Why were we born? Why are we here? What does life mean? The whole of Jesus' life is the answer to these questions so far as he was concerned, and these answers form many dramatic diagrams for living.

When Jesus was brought before Pilate, he was questioned concerning his activities and assertions. He answered, "To this end was I born, and for this cause came I into the world, that I should bear witness to the truth. Every one that is of the truth heareth my voice." And Pilate asked, "What is truth?" It is a good question. The search for Truth is unending, not merely by ecclesiastics, philosophers, and scholars, but by scientists too. Every time something "new" is discovered, another facet of Truth has been uncovered, another milestone on the road to Truth has been achieved. Perhaps we could define Absolute Truth as God Himself. All other truth is relative to that. Jesus came to bear witness to the Truth of God, and he spent his life demonstrating the power available to those who link their minds with that Truth.

Jesus did not have to come to earth at all. Unlike the rest of us, he chose to come back in order to do a great work for humanity, and therefore he is rightly called the savior of the world. Our spiritual and physical emancipation would have been much slower in coming had it not been for the work that Jesus did in and to the race mind.

In order to help us Jesus had to become one of us, he had to be born of a woman and come back into the human race. Nothing can be helped from the outside.

Even God does not help us from the outside. How does God heal us? How does God set us free from sin? How does He forgive us? Not from the outside, but by working in us, changing our consciousness. When the inner is changed, the outer change follows in accordance with that inner change.

Nothing can be saved from the outside and nothing can be destroyed from the outside. No country was ever destroyed from the outside. The Roman Empire was not destroyed by the barbarians; they only came in and took the loot. The Roman Empire was destroyed by deterioration within. Great institutions like great empires die from within. No church was ever destroyed by persecution. On the contrary, "the blood of the martyrs is the seed of the church." When a church dies, it dies from within.

We are told very little about Jesus' early life, but when he came on earth he necessarily had to lose most of his advanced consciousness for the time being, to become a baby. A small baby cannot possibly have the consciousness of a man, much less the consciousness that Jesus had before his incarnation. However, with Mary and Joseph as his earthly parents, he was brought up in the proper atmosphere and with the instruction that he needed. They were wise parents. In spite of their knowledge that he was a very special baby, they did not try to make a child genius out of him.

The first account of Jesus' youth was at age twelve, but his first awakening must have come around the age of seven, possibly a little earlier. The child would cease to be a baby. From then on there would be a continual unfoldment until at the age of puberty it dawned on him who he really was and why he had come. The Jews have their bar mitzvah and most of the Christian churches have some kind of confirmation—to correspond with that time when the child is deemed old enough to be responsible for his own spiritual life. So, one day when he was praying and meditating by himself, it suddenly dawned on the boy Jesus, and he remembered how he had planned this before his birth, how he had selected this work, and what lay ahead of him.

The first great opportunity came when his parents took him to Jerusalem for the feast of Passover. He found himself discussing important philosophical and religious questions with the learned doctors and scholars in the temple. "And all that heard him were astonished at his understanding and answers." Jesus' parents were a day's journey toward home before they noticed that he was missing. Retracing their steps, it was three days before they found him in the temple. And while they were amazed at the understanding their child displayed, they treated him just as any parents would handle an ordinary child. "Son," asked his mother, "why hast thou thus dealt with us? behold, thy father and I have sought thee sorrowing." And the account goes on to say that he returned to Nazareth with them, "and was subject unto them." Thus, in spite of his advanced understanding, he continued to be a well-disciplined child.

There has been much speculation about the hidden years of Jesus' life, the time between his first appearance in the temple and the beginning of his public work, a period of some eighteen years. The simple fact is that this time was spent in preparation. No great work is done without adequate preparation, and for the kind of work Jesus had come to do, much time and study was needed as well as hours and days spent in prayer and meditation. Jesus never felt he was too advanced to pray. There are those who get a smattering of the metaphysical teaching and feel if they make a couple of affirmations and the demonstration is not immediately forthcoming, they are ready to chuck the whole business. Not Jesus. Even after he began his public work, he was always praying.

So Jesus got the instruction he needed. He obviously had a greater depth than the teachers, but the good teacher can help the student to realize, control, and express his capacities. A good voice teacher can train a prima donna, though he may never have achieved fame as a singer himself. So there were people to teach Jesus. He traveled, became familiar with the great religions of his day, and began his public work when he was about thirty. He worked for three years, and then went away.

Jesus had great prophetic vision. He foresaw the present Aquarian Age and made indirect mention of it when his disciples were making preparation for that final Passover, which has become the Last Supper. He told them to follow the man with the waterpot—and the man with the waterpot, the gardener, is the symbol of this age. Jesus knew beforehand about what would take place around the crucifixion but not in detail. It turned out to be more difficult than he had expected, and he called upon Peter and James and John to help him. He was not infallible. And then he thought that the end of matter and limitation would come much sooner than was to be the case. But in spite of these seeming shortcomings, he was the greatest being who has come to earth up to now.

Jesus came to teach compassion and love of one another. He never wasted a moment in sad metaphysical speculation—the kind of thing that has done so much harm to India and other parts of Asia, the kind of thing which wasted so much time in the Middle Ages when serious-minded men argued how many angels could stand on the point of a needle. Jesus taught the higher metaphysics and the higher spirituality, and its cornerstone was compassion and love. Jesus said, "By this shall all men know that ye are my disciples, if ye have love one to another." When someone came to him and said, "Lord, we love you," he smiled and replied, "If ye love me, keep my commandments." If we keep his commandments, that is, if we follow his teaching and live the life, then are we his disciples. If we love one another in thought, word, and deed, then are we on our way to the manger, and the Star of the East is going ahead of us to show the way.

This is the story of the Christmas child. But how wrong it would be to think that the story ended two thousand years ago when Jesus dematerialized in what we call the Ascension. The truth is that the thing is going on all the time and that God means it for everyone. Jesus taught that there might be a Christ child born in every soul. "Behold, this child is set for the fall and rising again of many." God has no preferences. There are no reserved seats in heaven. We are all the same in His sight. We all have the same power and the same capacity. No outer ceremony makes any difference. No organization or person has any corner on this. It is your heart and the level of your consciousness that determines all.

If you keep your heart as the shepherds did, you will begin to know things that you cannot find in a book or a sermon. You will hear the heavenly choir, and the Christ child will be born and you will be there to receive it. After that, "Nothing can by any means hurt you."

CHAPTER 14

How To Un-Worry

*For the thing which I greatly feared is come upon me, and
that which I was afraid of is come unto me.*

JOB 3:25

T HE Book of Job is really a study in the origin
of evil, and in why things go wrong. Why do
you have pain and sickness? Why do you have
sorrows and regret? Why do you sometimes say or do
things that you are terribly sorry for afterward, and then
worry about how you are going to handle the situation?
The Book of Job undertakes to answer these questions.
If we understand why and how things happen, we are on
the road to learning how to handle them—how to un-
worry.

This book is one of the oldest parts of the Bible. It was
probably written by a great Arab sheik, an understanding
and spiritual man who had been asked by thoughtful
people why things go wrong. He had pondered long on
such questions as the origin of evil, why trouble comes to
people, and how they can make wrong things right. He

decided to put his ideas in the form of a play in which, under the inspiration of God, he dramatizes the things that trouble us, and the way to set them right.

The first act takes place in heaven where God is thought of as a big man with courtiers around and Satan as one of the leading characters. Satan in the Book of Job is not the devil of other parts of the Bible. He is a court official who goes out with the permission of the Lord and takes away all of Job's property. In the play Job is an enormously rich and influential Arab sheik. Most of his wealth would be in flocks and herds. They were taken away. Then his employees were killed, and finally his children were killed—seven sons and three daughters.

Obviously this is a parable and not history. It would be appalling to think that God, who is all-just, all-good, would slaughter these children to teach their father a lesson. The numbers seven and three are important. Here, seven means the seven main aspects of God, which Job had temporarily forgotten, so in effect they were taken away from him. The three daughters symbolize the three aspects of man: spirit, mind, and body. In other words, Job was thinking wrongly. He was judging by appearances instead of the Truth. Job later gave the key to his difficulties when he declared, "The thing which I greatly feared is come upon me." He was bringing more troubles on himself by his own wrong thinking.

Job was greatly stricken by the loss of all his property, but he continued to praise God. The Lord is supposed to have said to Satan, "There, didn't I tell you. Job is really a just man." And Satan replied, "Well, I'm not so sure. We have taken away all his property, but try hitting at the man. Strike at his body and then you will see a change in him." The body is an expression of both parts of our mentality, the conscious and subconscious. This is why it is important to demonstrate health. Since the body is the nearest part of our expression, we have to get it right. This is why Jesus stressed healing and why the Resurrection meant so much—complete dominion over the body.

So the Lord said to Satan, "We'll give Job another test. Strike at his body, but don't kill him." And Satan struck him with boils, so that Job was in a very bad way with his health. Even then he kept his faith in God, but he just managed to hang on. In utter misery he went out and sat on the ash heap. Isn't that a marvelous expression for depression and discouragement? Sitting on the ash heap? Isn't that just about the way people feel when they have great difficulties or when they are afraid? This Bible writer understood human nature. Sitting among ashes means a person is wallowing in his difficulties, surrounded by lost hopes, feeling terribly sorry for himself, and perhaps boring other people with his troubles. That is what Job did.

Then the play introduces Job's wife, and the author says that she was worse than Job. Instead of trying to comfort him, she goaded him and tried to drive out the last little bit of faith. She says to her husband, "Are you such a fool as still to believe in God? Curse God, and die." Remember, the woman in the Bible always represents the human soul, the human personality, and especially the feeling nature. The man represents the spiritual side, the Christ within. When things go wrong, it is usually our feelings that let us down, our feelings of fear and discouragement. "What's the use . . . Give up your faith in God . . . Prayer doesn't work." In the play the woman says it, but it was Job's own mind that was suggesting he turn away from God and let go of his faith. And then his higher self replies, "Thou speakest as one of the foolish women speaketh." He did not even lose his temper, and when one can keep his temper under control, he is still master of the situation.

However, Job had not yet risen high enough in consciousness to overcome his difficulties. He continued to sit out on the ash heap. Bad news travels fast and pretty soon his three friends came around. Job had been famous for his justice, wisdom, philanthropy, and fair dealing. His friends could not understand how a man with these qualities could be suffering as he was. Then one of them chided him, "Remember, I pray thee, whoever perished, being innocent? or where were the righteous cut off? . . . they that plow iniquity, and sow wickedness, reap the same." In other words, "We have pity for you but you must have been doing some evil things on the quiet." Nice friends!

Pity is always a bad thing. It is a counterfeit. The real thing is compassion. We should not see anyone suffer or in misery without trying to help him. To shrug our shoulders, walk away, and say "What can I do?" is wrong. The first thing we can do is to give him the right thought, to see the Christ in him, to pray for him. And if there is some practical thing we can do, we should do it. That is compassion, one of the shortest cuts into the kingdom of heaven. Jesus taught compassion in his parables, and demonstrated it in his life. He said, "I have compassion on the multitude."

Job's three friends represent the different ways in which we mull over a situation: "Why should this happen to me? I live a good clean life. I try to be fair in my dealings. I go to church. . . " We have all known good people who have contracted a serious illness or gotten into difficulties. And we have all asked the question, "Why do the righteous suffer?"

Then came a fourth friend, Elihu, who is described as
a young man. Spiritually, youth represents a readiness to
receive understanding. Young people are ready to hear
and do something new. This young man had studied the
Scriptures. He was more thoughtful than the others. He
could not believe that God would punish a man who had
been good. He looked for another reason. He said to
Job, "I don't think God is punishing you. God is testing
you for your own good."

That was a little better, but still not correct. God does
not need to test us. He already knows everything. It is we
who have to find out things, not God. Our temptations,
our misfortunes, do test us, but God does not send them.
When we make a mistake, or when a misfortune comes,
it is a test of our faith in God. If we stick to our faith, and
hold on in spite of appearances, we not only come
through, but we make a tremendous spiritual advance.

In the play Job's thoughts have been dramatized. His
lower self has been talking to him. He has been going
over and over in his mind the reasons for his predica-
ment until his mind is a whirlwind of confused and negative thinking. Then he gets his thought clear and out of
this whirlwind of confusion his higher self asserts itself.
It seems to him the Lord is speaking directly to him. He
is reminded of the majesty and grandeur of the universe.
"Canst thou bind the sweet influences of Pleiades, or loose
the bands of Orion? Canst thou bring forth Mazzaroth
in his season? or canst thou guide Arcturus with his sons?"

Mazzaroth means the signs of the Zodiac. The Zodiac
gives us about 26,000 years at a stretch, in segments of
about 2,000 years at a time. Stars always represent truth
that is beyond man's present apprehension. Even as we
understand more truth, there will always be more truth

to know. As natural science builds bigger telescopes and sees farther and farther into space, there are always more and more stars that come into view.

As Job contemplates the wonders of the universe, the thought strikes him, "Can I bind the sweet influences of Pleiades?" Can I change spiritual law? Of course we cannot change spiritual law, but we can change our reaction to it. We wouldn't really want to change spiritual law. It is the one guarantee of man's dominion. No matter what one may seem to have lost, no matter what mistakes one has made in the past, the spiritual law is there to save him, and to change everything into harmony and freedom and health.

There is no real freedom in self-will because self-will is a tyrant. The person who does anything he wants to do, whether right or wrong, has no free will at all. He is a slave to the cruelest master of all—the lower self. Freedom is found only by seeking spiritual law. "In His will is our peace." The Bible teaches that the Infinite Power, which created the heavenly bodies and maintains them in space, is waiting to work in your life, but only if you turn to that Power and allow it to work through you. By yourself, you cannot loose the bands of Orion—bondage to the animal forces within. You cannot guide Arcturus with his sons, but God can.

Man realizes, however dimly, that beyond those influences and propensities that seem to bind him so tightly to the flesh, there is something that is divine. There is some wonderful truth that is only faintly comprehended at this time. And at last in spiritual submission, he no longer struggles with that which he can only vaguely understand, but lets that Power work through him. It is thus, in recognition of his inescapable oneness with God, that the tide begins to turn.

Having begun to see the Truth, Job's higher self continues to reason with him. He is on the path of spiritual enlightenment and he now sees how much he did not understand before. Question after question comes into mind. The inner voice says, "Will the unicorn be willing to serve thee, or abide by thy crib? Canst thou bind the unicorn with his band in the furrow? or will he harrow the valleys after thee?" As long as we insist upon telling God His business, nothing very much can come of our prayers. When we dictate to God we are only using our own intellect and will; and how can they make us any better than we already are?

A man's problems arise because of some lack within him—and how can the same self that produced the problems overcome them? The ox, the mule, or even the donkey will obediently pull your plow and your cart and take them exactly where you want them to go; but you have to have a destination and know how to get there. The unicorn, on the other hand, will not do chores or follow a prescribed route. He knows where he is going, and you couldn't direct him because with your present consciousness you have never dreamed of such a place. But someday the unicorn will suddenly appear at your side, eyes flashing, nostrils quivering, pawing the ground with impatience. When that happens, do not try to put a bridle on him, or to look for some task for him to do. He will not do it, and there will not be time. No sooner does he appear than off he will go again. So do not pause to think twice, do not turn to look behind you. Leap upon his back, for he is a flying steed, and he will wing his way to the gates of the morning. On that ride problems are not solved—they are dissolved.

Why do things go wrong? The answer is: because of our false beliefs. The trouble with Job was false belief.

He didn't think so, although he had an inkling. He admitted that the things he greatly feared had come upon him. Yet he thought he was a model of spirituality. He was a good man, but he believed in evil. His children were fine children, but he was a possessive parent. He thought he owned them instead of thanking God for them and realizing they were God's children. He had never mentally cut the umbilical cord. He wanted to run their lives . . . and he suffered accordingly.

He believed that there were frightful diseases that could attack the body. He said in effect, "I will never get them, but they do exist"—and thus he got his pains and sores. He believed that his supply came from outer things—his flocks and herds—instead of from God. He confused the channel with the source, and the channel dried up as channels sometimes do.

This is why all those things happened to him—because of his erroneous beliefs. He had literally thought himself into trouble, and the only way to get out of it was to unthink his troubles. And when he began to unthink them, as the Bible says in its dramatic way, God spoke to him out of the whirlwind. He got his thought clear. The negative beliefs and false attitudes were swept away. He knew there was really nothing to worry about. He realized that these outer things only had the power he had been giving them in his thought. He cleared his thought, he got his inspiration. And as soon as he saw the Truth, his body was healed, and all his difficulties disappeared. He got back his property and his peace of mind.

The way to un-worry and put things right is to give up your belief in the appearance of things, no matter how distressing or unwelcome. Of course this is hard to do. Most of us have conditioned ourselves to accept the appearance at face value, and as long as we do this we will be filled with anxiety and worry. Job gave up his belief in trouble and limitation and things begin to come right.

There is a very important point in this story. Job had been very cross with his friends, indignant over their behavior toward him. On the surface he had every right to be, for they had accused him falsely. However, Job had learned his lesson. He now realized that feelings of anger and resentment would only bring more trouble, so he prayed for his friends. It was not until this step on his part that he made the complete demonstration.

We need to remember that if we are going to make wrong things right for ourselves, we have to think of helping our neighbor too. If we find the power to make life good for ourselves and pay no attention to the needs of our fellow man, then not only are we untrue to the Truth but we will lose what we have gained for ourselves. We cannot continue enjoying or receiving blessings unless we also give.

So Job prayed for his friends, and in the final act of the play, he found himself at peace with the world. The Lord gave him twice as much as he had before. He got 14,000 sheep, 6,000 camels, and so on. And God also gave him seven sons and three daughters to replace the ones he had lost. Children, in the Biblical sense, mean our works, our achievements. Thus the parable is saying that his good works went on again.

Then the family and relatives came round. Previously they had seemed aloof. And in the quaint old-world way the Bible says that everyone gave him a piece of money. A piece of money when he really needed peace of mind! There are people who think they have discharged their obligations to humanity if they hand a beggar a dime and tell him not to go and make a beast of himself. But there is a spiritual message here. Money means gold in this instance and gold means the omnipresence of God. That is what Job had *not* been believing. His relatives and friends probably did not know that, but it often happens that people are led to do things the reasons for which they are not aware of. They also brought an earring of gold. The ear symbolizes understanding, and Job had lacked that. To decorate the ear means to unfold the understanding.

In this parable of Job, as so often happens in the Bible, there is an extra dividend. It adds an interesting touch by giving the names of the three daughters. The first, Jemima, means a dove—which symbolizes the peace that comes with the inspiration of the Holy Spirit. When Jesus was baptized, the Holy Spirit was seen descending upon him in the form of a dove. The second name, Kezia, means acceptance. When you get your inspiration you must accept it, and to accept it means to express it. The third name is Kerenhappuch, which means born of pain, coming out of difficulty. When you pray you get your inspiration. You accept it and use it. You find your peace. Your troubles melt away. Good things come out of pain and difficulty. Wrong things become right.

Whatever happens to you, lift up your heart, because if you hold on to your faith your liberation is very nigh. If you go through the difficulty in faith, you will be far, far above your present level when the demonstration comes. God blesses the latter end more than the beginning.

Bible literally, whereas Divine Providence meant it to be taken as parable.

Jesus excelled all others in the teaching of Truth through parable. It is one of the ironies of fate that, being one of the greatest of all literary men, Jesus Christ never wrote a word except once when he wrote with his finger in the dust. He was one of the greatest short-story writers of all times, and whoever reads one of his parables feels himself touched because there is a quality in them quite unlike anything else in literature. For instance, the story of the Prodigal Son has no equal. It has color, feeling, lovingness, drama, in addition to the metaphysical truth that we seldom get elsewhere. It seems to sum up the whole story of your life and mine and of all mankind. If all else in the Bible should be lost, the story of the Prodigal Son would itself give the basic message of the Bible.

Living in patriarchal times was this man of vast property. He had two sons, and as often happens in families, the two sons were very much unlike. Has it ever struck you how Providence has made brothers, and sisters too, so exceedingly unlike in character? Not only unlike physically—one with the Jones cast in his eye, the other with the Robinson walk—but very unlike in personality and character. Providence has arranged it that way because different people have different lessons to learn. They are sent, or gravitate, to certain families in order to learn the discipline that those particular families will give them.

In the story the elder brother realizes his oneness with his father. He realizes the goodness of his father and the goodness of things in general, and he stays with his father. But the younger brother is different. He thinks that he will set up in business for himself. He feels restricted by the ancestral home, and he thinks to himself, "Now I will go out and do a bit of exploring on my own account."

Many of us can identify with this younger son because usually we have the urge to go out and do something new. We do not feel we have to follow in the footsteps of our father. We are not satisfied with the status quo.

The younger son came to his father and said, "I know I shall get my inheritance someday, but I would like to have it now, if you don't mind." The father, being very wise, did not argue with him. The one thing you should never do is preach a sermon to the young people. Let them go to church for that, and at least they won't have a chance to blame it on you! So the father said, "Very well, here is your share, go ahead." The young man went forth, but when he got out he did not find it quite as he had expected. Things took on a different aspect. He did not start the great work he had planned when he was home. He spent his capital on all kinds of foolishness. He bought a lot of things he did not really want and got no happiness from them. He fell into melancholy ways, because the most melancholy thing in the world is what is called "having a good time." How very much suffering is summed up in people "having a good time"!

Finally, his money was gone, his fair-weather friends had left him, and he had lost contact with his father. From a comfortable home and a place of respect in the community he had descended to being a swineherd, and to the Hebrew there was nothing lower. In a way it is no worse than having to look after cows or other animals, but to the Hebrew it was a terrible thing because they considered the pig unclean and a curse. So the young son had come down to the very lowest status.

There he was in a foreign country, among strangers, with nothing left—not even his self-respect. And then something happened: a thought came to him. He found himself saying, "I will arise and go unto my father." Where did that come from? From the Prodigal Son? No. He could not do it. The only thing he could do was to go into low company, make a fool of himself and do a thorough job of it. It was the direct inspiration of God, leading him to say, "I will arise and go unto my father." Up to that time he probably had thought over his plight many times, and each time doubts and fears would arise. "I don't think my father would take me back. I don't deserve it. It's too late now."

But when he came to himself—and that means coming to your higher self—when he listened to the voice of God, he heard himself saying, "I will arise and go unto my father." So he did. And the Bible tells us that when he got home, the father came out to meet him. That meant more in the Oriental world than it would today. This great landowner was used to servants doing his bidding. He was a patriarch and people would come to him. But he was so happy to have his son back that when the son was a long way off, the father ran out to meet him, embraced him, and probably kissed him on both cheeks.

Then we are told in this wonderful Oriental style how the father gave a great feast for him. A feast meant more in those days than it does today. So many people today are on diets or contemplating going on a diet that we are not so free and easy with our feasts. This feast was the real thing, with singing and dancing and the fatted calf that had been killed for the occasion.

Now the elder brother was the good boy of the family. He had stayed home, and of course in consequence of being good and having stayed at home, he felt mighty virtuous. One hesitates to say there is danger in virtue, but there is. The danger is that it makes people *feel* superior. When you catch yourself feeling very virtuous, be careful, because you are walking on dangerous ground.

This brother felt very virtuous, and when he heard the music and saw the lights flashing in the garden, he said to one of the servants, "What is all this?" And the servant replied, "Don't you know? Your brother has come back and we are having a party. I killed the fatted calf this morning." And this virtuous person, the elder son, became very angry. You see, he was not really so virtuous as he thought. Virtuous people seldom are. In his anger, he rushed to his father and said, "What is the meaning of all this? I have been home working all the while and nothing like this was done for me! I have been looking after my family's welfare, and have got nothing for it but my room and board, but this fellow goes out and misbehaves outrageously, spends all his money, and instead of kicking him you give him a feast!" The father simply replied, "Son, thou art ever with me, and all that I have is thine."

Now, the Bible is written in such a way that no matter on what level of understanding a person may be, there will be a message for him. Jesus told the story in this way so that those who are not ready for the deeper understanding would still get the lesson that it is never too late to pray. They would realize that they are never so far from God that He will not receive them back. Millions of people are ready for that lesson who are not ready for the deeper thing—but both lessons are true.

The deeper lesson is that each one of these sons represents each one of us. The elder son is our higher nature, and the son who went out is our lower nature. As a rule, it is not until we have gotten into difficulties, suffered fear, doubt, defeat, sickness, or positive misfortune, either with ourselves or with someone we love, that we turn and go back to God. Meanwhile, the higher self, the self that knows the Truth but sometimes forgets it—that self is still with the Father.

Often, like the Prodigal Son, we believe the Truth. We are, for the time being, in our Father's house, but there comes a time when we let the lower self, our selfish desires and emotions, beguile us into going off to a "strange country." For a time the newfound freedom seems wonderful. And then little by little we begin to realize that by leaving the Father, we have cut off our power. We have separated ourselves from the Source of our abundance and well-being. Fear and doubt creep in to produce more difficulties.

And then, having tried everything else, the thought comes to pray and turn once more to Him, and we say, "I will arise and go unto my father." To our surprise, God doesn't say, "Well, you have kept me waiting. Now I will keep you waiting." No, we find that God comes out to meet us. One of the most beautiful things in the Bible is the statement "When he was yet a long way off, his father saw him, and had compassion, and ran, and fell on his neck, and kissed him." God is always ready to meet us more than halfway. The fear is dissolved, the problem is solved, and once more we have the sense of unity with Him.

That is the story of the Prodigal Son and that is really the story of everyone at one time or another. Whenever we have a problem or difficulty, whenever we are fearful or depressed and assailed by doubt, the moment we think "I will pray. I will treat"—that is the voice of God whispering to us to turn to Him. And then perhaps the lower self says, "What's the use . . . I couldn't demonstrate that now . . . It's too much to expect . . . I'm not ready." This is still the husks and the swine.

And then the voice of God comes again and says, "Now is the accepted time; now is the day of salvation. . . . Look unto me, and be ye saved, all the ends of the earth." And finally the prodigal comes to himself. He realizes how many there are in his Father's house who have bread enough and to spare, and he says, "I will arise and go unto my Father. I am not worthy but I know He will listen. He'll take care of me." And, of course, God always does.

The people who get peace of mind, freedom, joy, and prosperity are the simple-hearted people, the people who take God at His word without analyzing or subtlety. One can analyze a rose. He can tear it apart petal by petal but of course he will no longer have a rose. And when you analyze God, you have lost God. When we go to God frankly and sincerely, everything is cleared up. There are no reservations when God works. Divine and complete harmony awaits us when we "arise and go unto the Father."

But the meaning in this parable goes even deeper than this because it is a treatise on the nature of man. It conceals the three great issues of life. We are told that when the Prodigal Son came back, his father not only received him in love and forgiveness, but he turned to his servants and said, "Bring forth the best robe, and put it on him; and put a ring on his hand, and shoes on his feet." It is a wonderful picture of Oriental formality. He wanted all the household to know that his son was re-established. That was the way they did it, with ceremony and feasting and dancing and rejoicing.

The three things—the robe, the ring, and the shoes— represent the three great issues of life, thus giving a deep metaphysical meaning to the story. The robe represents the right attitude of mind—right thinking, right knowing, right action. The right attitude of mind means the constructive attitude, the victorious attitude, the attitude of mind that realizes that behind every appearance, no matter how distressing, there is the Truth. That is the attitude of mind that heals, for it sees the presence of God everywhere.

Elsewhere the Bible speaks of "robes of righteousness," and in Revelation it speaks of those who have come through difficulties by means of prayer as having their robes washed white in the blood of the Lamb. This is a figurative expression meaning that by turning to God and realizing His goodness and our unity with Him, the lower things in our nature begin to melt away. That is the robe.

The next thing they gave the Prodigal Son was a ring. A ring was put on his hand, symbolizing spiritual unity. That is why a ring is used in marriage. In this parable the ring symbolizes that we are one with God and we know it. We no longer have any reason to feel that we are the prodigal among the husks. We are not only received back and made His son again, but we are reunited with Him. We no longer are merely depending upon ourselves, but we know that "in him we live and move and have our being." It means that there cannot be any lack anywhere, for we live in a continuum of ever-present divine abundance, and we bring it into existence by reminding ourselves of our unity with God.

Finally, they put shoes on his feet. Feet always represent understanding, and here we have that understanding protected against error and doubt. When we really understand a thing, we are protected against being mistaken about it. For example, when we really know that two and two make four, then we are protected against the mistake of thinking that two and two make five. So knowledge is protection against misunderstanding.

Divine understanding is achieved through right thinking and knowledge of our unity with God. Thus these three great issues give us dominion. Moses, you will remember, was told to take off his shoes when he came into the presence of God. Through long prayer and communion with God he had arrived at the point of dominion where he knew that the place whereon he stood was "holy ground." He had achieved conscious union with God where he could take off his shoes. He no longer needed protection for his understanding. He knew there was no place where God is not. Thus, he was always standing on holy ground.

There is one other point in connection with the story of the Prodigal Son. It concerns the elder son. Almost everyone understands the younger son to some extent, but the elder son is not understood. Jesus knew this. The mistake of the elder son boils down to this: he feels he is one with the father but he misses his own individuality, or is afraid of it. He knows that all that the father has is his, but he lacks the courage to do anything with it. Although he is aware of his divine relationship and its implication, he never has the gumption to do anything on his own initiative. He is angry when he sees his younger brother wasting his substance, but he never has the spiritual enterprise to use it in a good way himself.

So it is with many people, especially those who know something of Truth. They sit down quietly with the knowledge of being one with God and then never attempt to demonstrate it. You must use this metaphysical tool that you have forged in consciousness. You must do something with your metaphysical knowledge besides just possessing it. If you think you possess it and do not use it, then you do not really have it.

The fault of the elder son is his self-righteousness and what we might call his negative goodness. It is all knife and nothing to cut. At some point in your spiritual growth you cease to do the most obvious and wicked things because you are getting higher in consciousness. You understand the law of Karma. You know you cannot accumulate understanding as you might pile up dimes in a piggy bank or stamps in an album, no more than the elder son could accumulate wealth in his father's house. Unless you make use of the understanding you possess today, you will not get any more tomorrow. The reason you do not have any more spiritual understanding than you have today is because you did not use what you had to the fullest degree yesterday. Understanding, like all spiritual power, increases with use.

That is why Jesus points out in the parable of the Ten Talents that the master said to his servant who had received five talents and then doubled them, "Thou hast been faithful over a few things, I will make thee ruler over many things."

CHAPTER 16

Shipwreck

For there stood by me this night the angel of God, whose I am, and whom I serve, saying, Fear not, Paul; thou must be brought before Caesar: and, lo, God hath given thee all them that sail with thee.

ACTS 27:23, 24

THIS chapter is one of the most interesting chapters in the Bible, not especially important spiritually, but of extraordinary human interest. It reveals the literary power of the Bible at one of its heights. It is a wonderful story of a sea voyage and a thrilling shipwreck in the Old World nineteen hundred years ago. As a piece of literature, I maintain that it is unsurpassed. I know of nothing in Marryat or Stevenson or Conrad or any of the other sea writers that is more vivid and real.

To set the stage, we must give a little background on the main character of the story, Paul. Thank God we are getting away from the old view that the people in the Bible were supermen who had nothing in common with us. If you read the Bible account of Abraham, you see what a very human person he was. The Bible also reveals that Moses began on a very low level. He was confused, made mistakes, contradicted himself, and gradually worked through that. Eventually he got more understanding, more illumination, and finally made his reunion with God—which is the goal of all spiritual unfoldment—that place where you are a pillar in the house of God and need go out no more unless you want to.

Right through the Bible we read of people like Samson and Samuel and Elijah, and always it is the same story, people awakening slowly to the importance of spiritual things, grasping a little of it, making mistakes; paying for the mistake, working through it, a little more light, another mistake, more light, fewer mistakes, more and more light, and finally the triumph.

We find the same thing with Paul. He had the problem of so many today, a defect of disposition. Paul did not deliberately do wrong. Almost from boyhood, Paul would rather have been burned at the stake than to have committed deliberate sin. But he had a disposition that made him constantly "kick against the pricks." When we make these mistakes, of course we have to pay for them. Not that God punishes us; it is the natural working out of the law—for every action there is a corresponding reaction.

Paul had wanted to serve God, so he went out and persecuted Jesus Christ. Jesus was dedicating his life to spreading the truth about God and doing God's will, and Paul persecuted his followers. He had to pay for this . . . and later he had a change of heart, he saw the light. Because Paul was one of the greatest of the sons of men, when he saw he was in the wrong, he had the courage and humility to admit it and go straight over to the other side. I wonder how many people have ever realized what it must have cost Paul to come out in front of his own people where he held such a distinguished place and admit that he had been wrong. Only the truly great can acknowledge their mistakes. Paul was one of them. He openly admitted that these followers of Jesus, who were so much despised, were right; and he broke with everything and threw in his lot with them.

Paul's life is a study in man's quest for spiritual growth. He was constantly up against a fault in his own disposition. It would cause him terrible pain and suffering for a time, but then he would overcome it and take a step higher. He was on the spiritual path, seeking God each day, and each day he got nearer to God. There was nothing in the world that could keep Paul away from God except his own faults of disposition.

We all know people who would not deliberately do wrong, who would not tell a lie or even take a penny dishonestly, yet who have obvious faults of disposition—obvious to their friends, not to themselves—and these are the only things that stand between them and God. A fault of disposition, of which you are not aware or that you only dimly suspect, may be the only thing that is keeping you from complete unity with God—which means keeping you from health, freedom, happiness, peace of mind, and your heart's desire. In many people it is not overt sin or even want of an intellectual comprehension of Truth, but it is a fault of disposition that prevents that which is intellectually apprehended from being made into spiritual experience. This was Paul's "thorn in the side."

Paul was preaching and teaching around the Mediterranean, which was the center of the Old World. Because Rome considered the Christian movement an insurgency, he was arrested. Now Paul was a Roman citizen, and because he was stubborn with that rigidity of disposition and intense spiritual pride and pigheadedness (there is no other word to describe that defect in Paul's character), he appealed to Caesar.

Until he got his full illumination, Paul was the complete and perfect snob. This was what Paul had to meet within his own heart. He was intensely proud of his pure Hebrew descent. He had a half-conscious contempt for all Gentiles. He was extremely proud that he came of the tribe of Benjamin, and he thought that all the other Hebrews were a little inferior to him. If they were the chosen race, then Benjamin was the chosen tribe. But he was not only a Benjamite, he was a Pharisee, and if the Benjamites were the chosen tribe, the Benjamite Pharaisees were the real chosen people. And among that particular little clique there was one chosen above all, and that was Paul of Tarsus.

All this reveals Paul's problem of disposition to be overcome in his spiritual quest. And on top of this he was a Roman citizen, that is to say, he had full legal rights in the Roman Empire. He was inordinately proud of this, although he should not have been if he were so proud of being a Hebrew, a Benjamite, etc. However, in that Old World it gave a man great status to be a Roman citizen, and with all his striving and desire for spiritual things, Paul could not forego the status symbol. Later he overcame all these things. They almost tore him to pieces. They almost broke his heart, as faults of disposition do, but he overcame them ultimately. In the meantime, he had to suffer much because of them.

So Paul was arrested for his Christian activities. At a certain point in the proceedings the magistrate, whom Paul considered to be very much his inferior, said something, and Paul threw out his chest and replied, "I am a Roman citizen and I appeal to Caesar." The Bible tells us that if he had not appealed to Caesar he could have been set free. Paul should have known the law that when you appeal in that way to Caesar, to Caesar you have to go and God Himself will not save you from it.

You have self-determination, and when you appeal to Caesar, to Caesar you will go. Jesus put the same thought in another way: "All they that take the sword shall perish with the sword." How many Christians during nineteen centuries have really thought what this means? They say Jesus was God and they worship him and say they are good Christians; but as for the things he said, they do not pay the slightest attention. Jesus refers not only to a sword of steel. He is talking about any mental attitude that you take up in your life. In other words, you will have to meet the consequences of what you think or speak or do. When you appeal to Caesar, to Caesar you will go. It will not be any good saying, "I didn't mean it . . . That wasn't my intention . . . You have misunderstood me." The Great Law of Being knows you thoroughly and never misunderstands you.

So Paul said, "I appeal to Caesar," and to Caesar he went. A detail of soldiers under a centurion was set aside to take charge of him. The centurion seems to have been a decent, matter-of-fact type of man. He probably looked upon Paul as a fanatic, but he recognized Paul's basic goodness. The outstanding quality in the Roman character was that rather shortsighted but very efficient, matter-of-fact, no-darned-nonsense-about-me attitude of mind. This was the Roman outlook that enabled the people to do so many things with bridges and aqueducts and roads, and so few things in other important areas of human relationships and needs.

This centurion took Paul into custody and then had to arrange to get him to Rome. Communications in the

Mediterranean were extremely good in the Roman Empire, as good as they were going to be for another eighteen hundred years. Travelers went around the Mediterranean in small ships that were quite good for their purpose and for their time, though a little more knowledge of physics would have made them much handier to manage. The seamen of that day were very good with the power at their disposal.

We are told in this chapter how the centurion and his men first took Paul here and then there, and finally they got a boat that was starting out for Rome. There were about 276 persons on board: the crew, the soldiers under the centurion, and a number of prisoners. So it was a fair-sized boat. Paul was there as a prisoner, of course, but he was treated with great respect. The Roman centurion was a pagan, but he was a gentleman, and he treated his prisoner with great consideration. The hallmark of a gentleman is that he never takes advantage of someone who is in a difficult or inferior position.

The party set sail but not without protest from Paul. He foresaw that there would be difficulties, and he advised them not to sail. He said, "I perceive that this voyage will be with hurt and much damage, not only of the lading and ship, but also of our lives." Of course they would not listen to him. After all, he was a landlubber and obviously a "crank" anyway. What did a rabbi or teacher know about the sea? A religious teacher is sure to be a general fool and to know nothing about the world! And so they paid no attention to him.

Read this 27th chapter of the Acts of the Apostles. It is a marvelous description of a storm at sea that, as I have said, is probably unsurpassed in literature. I wonder why people who undertake to teach the Bible to children, and especially to boys, do not read this chapter to them.

I think it would prejudice a boy in favor of the Bible for the rest of his life.

There was a very rough storm and presently they had to throw the cargo overboard. Then they began to throw the ropes and tackle overboard to lighten the ship. They talked about throwing the prisoners overboard too, they were so scared. When people are frightened they are often cruel. Cruelty is almost always the outcome of fear. Wherever you come across a case of cruelty, whether it is individual cruelty, persecution of a particular group by other people, or national cruelty, always there is fear. Fear is cruel, just as love is always kind and healing and liberating.

However, the centurion would not allow that. The storm continued, and the account says, "When neither sun nor stars in many days appeared, and no small tempest lay on us, all hope that we should be saved was then taken away."

Paul sought God every day, and at this period he got his realization each day. And although to mortal eye all seemed hopeless, Paul stood up in the midst of the group and said, "I exhort you to be of good cheer: for there shall be no loss of any man's life among you, but of the ship. For there stood by me this night the angel of God, whose I am, and whom I serve, saying, 'Fear not, Paul; thou must be brought before Caesar: and, lo, God hath given thee all them that sail with thee.' Wherefore, sirs, be of good cheer: for I believe God, that it shall be even as it was told me."

Paul to some extent had the faculty of reading the future, a faculty that belongs to the seer and to those who are diligently seeking God. He knew pretty well what was going to happen within the next few days. Then the sailors, disregarding the tradition of the sea, were going to desert the ship and leave the others. The law of the sea is that the sailor always tries to save his passengers first. Paul read their minds. Knowing what they were thinking, he told the soldiers that the sailors were going to pretend they were getting into a boat to drop some anchors. He said, "Don't let them go or we all shall perish." The soldiers cut the rope and the boat fell into the sea.

Finally they came to an estuary and tried to save the ship by running it hard aground, but the waves were so great that the forepart of the ship stuck fast and the hinder part was smashed to pieces. Those who could swim jumped out and swam to the shore. The others got on boards and pieces of wreckage, and finally they all got ashore. It is a wonderful story. If you read it carefully you can almost hear the howling of the wind in the tackle and feel the rocking of the ship.

Paul finally got to Rome full of his own ideas and interpretations, talking a lot about Jesus Christ—but usually putting Paul first and Jesus second. If one studies the life of Paul carefully with a fresh mind, putting aside what some preacher said years ago, he will find it to be an extraordinarily interesting study in human nature. And he will become aware of Paul's continuing battle with his own desires and his frightful egotism. Of course this is not unique with Paul. The besetting sin of religious people, particularly the leaders, has usually been a gnawing egotism that marks most of their lives. Perhaps that is why they seek so hard to find God. Subconsciously they feel that that egotism is the very devil itself and they must escape at all costs. Normally, as the years go on, it gets less and less, and in most cases there is a final and beautiful triumph when the ego is overcome and God comes first.

Thus it was with Paul. Paul finally got to the place where God was really first, and the teachings of Jesus Christ came first, last, and all the time. But this was not easily accomplished. Almost to the very end when he laid down his life for his principles the "thorn" was with him.

If a great soul like Paul had to meet this defect of disposition, how much more are we lesser souls likely to have our lives shipwrecked by faults of character. Moses came very near wrecking his life through a fault of disposition. There are others mentioned in the Bible, and there are great seers and saints outside the Bible, like Gandhi, St. Augustine, and St. Theresa, who have been troubled in the same way. Dwight L. Moody, the evangelist, said, "My greatest problem is Dwight L. Moody." As we delve into the lives of these great men and women, and particularly when we study Paul, we realize that the thing we need most to work upon is probably some defect in disposition, some fault of character that is holding us back. Probably we need more than anything else to appeal to God for wisdom, intelligence, and more understanding in our hearts. Nothing will enable us to achieve this but the direct action of the grace of God in our souls. If we rely upon the intellect, so-called common sense, we shall fool ourselves the whole time.

Jeremiah says, "The heart is deceitful above all things, and desperately wicked: who can know it?" This means that it is so extraordinarily easy for human beings to deceive themselves that very few people really come to a clear understanding of their own dispositions and their own hearts. Very few people are really aware of the fault that most keeps them back. All of us are aware of many faults in ourselves, yes, but probably the thing that keeps us back most, the thing that brings most of the grief into our lives, we seldom suspect.

Robert Burns said, "O would some power the giftie gi'e us / To see ourselves as others see us." We need to go a step beyond that and claim that God is giving us the power to see ourselves as we really are. It would be a shock in a good many cases. Most of us have built up an imaginary figure, the thing that we want to live with. We do not make this figure perfect because we could not accept it if we did. We say, "Well, of course, he has his faults and failings. Who hasn't? But on the whole he is a pretty darned good fellow and there are many worse than he is," etc. That is the natural human way, but we have to destroy that built-up figure. That synthetic lie about ourselves has to be discarded if we really mean business. We have to claim the light of God to see ourselves as we really are. And no matter what we see, the power of God can change it.

Isn't it better to know the worst? The person who is afraid of a diagnosis is not facing up to his difficulty. He is sick and he knows it. He has pain but he cannot face the doctor for his diagnosis. When I tell these people to go to the doctor, they say, "But I don't want him to tell me that I have thus and so." I say, "You have either got it or you haven't. Seeing the doctor won't give it to you. If you really have a bad heart condition, or whatever it is, you have got it, and the doctor by examining you cannot give it to you. Probably he will say you haven't got it, but if you have, you had better know it. Know what is there and you can spiritually treat it."

So it is with the moral and spiritual condition of our hearts. We had better see what is there and face up to it. Then we can take steps to meet it. Otherwise people go on fooling themselves. In my work I have come across many men and women whose main and continuing problem was a fault of disposition, yet who did not even faintly suspect such was the case.

One man came to consult me who was having great difficulty in his business life. Opportunities would seem to open up, but when the time came to sign the contract or undertake a particular piece of business the deal would fall through. The real difficulty turned out to be within himself. Because of feelings of inferiority concerning his personal appearance, he unconsciously took an over-aggressive attitude toward people and toward situations, and this was spoiling things for him.

Sometimes it is a know-it-all attitude. An actress of considerable talent who was doing very well in her professional career found that it was very difficult for her to keep friends. Again the difficulty was within herself. She was extremely opinionated about things and she was constantly getting into arguments with others. When I said to her, "Why don't you, as a matter of policy, let the other fellow win some of the arguments, or better still, why get into an argument at all?" she replied, "But what I say is true." I said, "That may be the case, but you are losing friends through your attitude." After some further counseling and spiritual treatment, she saw the light, and from then on her personal life began to improve.

There are many more common defects of personality that hold people back, such as constant faultfinding and criticism, or giving an "organ recital" in response to the greeting "How are you?" I know people who imagine themselves to be on the spiritual path, but it is perfectly obvious to others that they have certain mental habits and faults of disposition that make the thing impossible. Yet they themselves do not suspect it. If they went out picking pockets it would be obvious to them that picking pockets would not go with the spiritual life. The faults of disposition that destroy us are not so obvious.

Sometimes you hear one person say about another, "I have a good mind to tell him about that." It is seldom any use. It probably would not be well received, or if it were well received, it would not be understood.

If you feel that there is something in your personality that should not be there, or if you suspect that there is something that ought to be changed and you do not know what, claim every day that God is Light, that God is not only Life and Truth and Love and the other qualities, but God is Light, and light means knowledge and understanding. Claim, "God illumines my soul so that I see it as it is."

Do not ask your friends about it or discuss it with the family. If you need outside help, go to a good spiritual counselor, but prepare yourself spiritually as outlined above. Then whatever advice you get you will perceive with spiritual understanding, and it will be much easier to accept the change that will be necessary.

When Paul at last realized his own difficulties of temperament and disposition, he probably had a bad time for a while. In spite of the angel that stood by him in the shipwreck, in spite of the sacrifices he had made for the teaching of Jesus Christ, in spite of the wonderful things that he already was, yet when he got his illumination of self, he probably was appalled for a time. But that disappeared as the Power of God continued to work through him. That Power will not be any less with us if we are willing to face up to our faults of disposition.

Paul went through the shipwreck, which is symbolic of the danger of all kinds of shipwrecks in the soul. The angel of God stood by Paul because Paul was a praying man. He thoroughly believed in God even though at times he let his personality get between himself and the Light. But when the test came Paul turned sincerely to

God and got his inspiration. And God will do the same for us whenever we sincerely turn to Him without reservation. However, if you insist upon appealing to Caesar, then of course to Caesar you will have to go, and that only means more heartbreak, delay, and disappointment.

CHAPTER 17

The Second Coming of the Christ

The Lord Jesus shall be revealed from heaven with his mighty angels, in flaming fire taking vengeance on them that know not God, and that obey not the gospel of our Lord Jesus Christ: who shall be punished with everlasting destruction from the presence of the Lord, and from the glory of his power.

II THESSALOSNIANS: 1:7–9

IN all the ages and in all countries where the Christian message is known, men and women have looked, generation after generation, for the second coming of the Christ. None of the Gospels were written while Jesus was on earth, and the reason is that the early Christians were looking for the almost immediate personal return of Jesus Christ. Since that time people all over the world have continued to look for his return in the flesh. It is this very thing that has prevented the real second coming of the Christ in the world hundreds of years ago.

Jesus Christ never taught his followers to look to his personality and to worship him. On the contrary, he labored year after year to get the people to accept his *teaching* and to look away from himself to an impersonal and incorporeal God in the universe Who manifests in man—that which he lovingly called "the Father within." In fact, Jesus made it plain that unless he left them, the Holy Spirit would not come. As long as people looked to a person or an institution, a man or a church, they were missing the divine thing within themselves.

If Jesus had not done what he did in Holy Week, as it is rightly called, and then on Calvary, and over the Easter weekend, and during his post-Easter sojourn, the human race would have had to wait thousands of years longer for true salvation and that sense of true dominion that comes with the second coming of the Christ. He dematerialized his body in that cave where it was laid. He did that by his thought, and it meant that he definitely had had to overcome a subconscious belief in the power of matter. Having been born into the human race he had acquired certain false beliefs from the race mind, just as we all have accepted false beliefs from the race mind.

Whenever we pray, whenever we spiritualize our thought, we are getting away from the bondage of matter, and we are lifting the race mind a tiny fraction too. What Jesus did was of great magnitude. Consequently, he was able to overcome any belief in the power of matter and therefore he was able to melt his body back into the ether, or, as modern science calls it, energy. Today physical science teaches that matter is really little whirlpools of energy. Energy and matter are not the separate things we used to be taught. Science is getting closer to the truth that there is but one all-pervading substance. Some may call it ether; others may call it energy. The name does not matter. There is one divine substance and all things are made of that.

Having demonstrated his power over matter and the physical body, Jesus was able to appear to his disciples and friends on a number of occasions after his resurrection. The Bible says it was forty days, and forty in the Bible symbology means an indefinite length of time, usually a matter of weeks. Jesus stayed with them, teaching them and getting them ready for the work that they were to do.

The Bible keeps emphasizing their lack of understanding. We are told that on the road to Emmaus they did not recognize him even when he expounded the Scriptures to them, beginning with Moses and coming up through the prophets and Psalms. We are all guilty of that sort of thing. We hear but we do not always understand. We see and yet we see not. We misinterpret, not just Biblical things, but the actions and motivations of others. However, Jesus knew the shortcomings of his Apostles and he loved them in spite of those shortcomings. His problem, therefore, was to teach them as much as he could before he had to go away and not return.

When Jesus finally went away, for the first time his apostles, students, and friends were thrown back on their own resources. They could no longer turn to him and say, "Oh, the master will do it." There are many who have to be weaned away from reliance on others. Often we become so attached to a teacher, a friend, an employer, a father or mother, and even a job, that we are unable to stand on our own. All the great teachers in every branch of knowledge have said, "Don't rely on me, rely on the teaching." And yet the students go on relying on the teacher. Jesus knew this, and he knew that unless he personally went away his apostles would never do the great work he wanted them to do. Henry Ward Beecher, the eminent Brooklyn preacher, once said, "Don't do as I do, but do as I say." He was emphasizing this very point, the thing that Jesus repeatedly stressed: each one must get his own contact with God.

This is why Jesus told his disciples a short time before he made the Ascension demonstration, "Tarry ye in the city of Jerusalem, until ye be endued with power from on high." They happened to be near Jerusalem at the time, but Jesus meant something more than the material city. We are taking the esoteric meaning of the Bible, which gives us keys to our daily living. Jerusalem means that state of mind where we are praying and waiting upon God, where we have a sense of peace but have not yet got any sense of realization. When you get the realization the Bible calls that Mt. Zion. But when you have not yet got it and are looking for it, that is Jerusalem. So in effect Jesus was saying, "You must wait until you get some sense of the presence of God. You must find the Christ for yourselves. Then you will really understand from an inner teaching what you now grasp only with your conscious mind." To tarry in Jerusalem is to keep the high watch until you get a sense of the presence of God and the Christ becomes a living factor in your heart.

The disciples did tarry in Jerusalem. They sought the Christ at first hand, and from the day they found him the things that Jesus taught became alive within them. And then they went out and worked the miracles that changed the history of the world.

So Jesus went away. He transcended, dematerialized, rose in consciousness above the limitations of the three-dimensional plane in which we live, and disappeared. Then, when his followers came together of one accord and in one place, on what we call the Day of Pentecost, the second coming of the Christ took place for those who were ready to receive it on that day. It was the day when they got their own personal, living, divine contact with God. It seemed to them like tongues of fire lighting on each one. Fire in the Bible signifies the cleansing action of the Holy Spirit. All the old limiting ideas were wiped out of their consciousness and they were "set on fire" with the idea of going out and giving the gospel— the good news—to the world.

That was the second coming of the Christ for the disciples. Having received the second coming of the Christ, which is also called "the baptism of the Holy Spirit," these simple, everyday men like us went out and turned the world upside down, performing miracles that still influence the course of human history. And from that day to this, all through history, wherever people have been ready to accept that message and to strive for that experience, the second coming of the Christ has been there for those particular individuals to receive.

We have now reached a stage in the history of the world when the whole of the human race as a body, or at least a large majority of people of every kind and of every race, are ready for the second coming of the Christ; and it is because the general public is ready to receive this wonderful thing that it is beginning to happen. God is outside of space and time, and the Christ power of God, which has existed throughout all eternity, has always been ready if only the human race had been ready to receive it.

Jesus foresaw that as the Old Age waned and the New Age approached, all sorts of external happenings would be seen on the face of the earth. And this is dramatically taking place. Human destiny has turned a corner. We have had the greatest wars in history. We have had the greatest political revolutions in history. The old Czarist empire, the German empire, the British empire, the ancient Chinese empire, have all been swept away. Monarchies have fallen. The whole of Europe has been turned upside down, as well as the greater part of Asia and Africa. Never before in history has there been so vast a political upheaval. This is because of the change in the race mentality, making it possible for the second coming of the Christ that is taking place now in the hearts of hundreds of thousands of people.

Jesus foresaw all this, and the Bible calls it "the last days," meaning the end of the Old Age. It does not mean that our planet, the earth, is going to burn up or disappear, but it does mean that the old limited ideas concerning God and man are coming to an end.

It is one's idea of God that controls his whole life. It is the idea that he has of God that governs the kind of health he has, the sort of business he is in, the kind of city he lives in, the type of government he has.

It is man's concept of God that governs his life from beginning to end. Even those who profess no God will find their lives governed by *that concept* concerning God. However, never before this present age, with the exception of the prophets of old, has man's concept of God risen to such heights, nor risen so rapidly. It is because of this transition from the old to the new that we see so much confusion and turmoil in the world. And with the individual, when the Christ of God has been born in his soul, the whole outer picture will have begun to break up.

The mystics, those wise ones of ancient times, testified that when any man or woman gets a larger concept of God, then his or her personal affairs will change for the better, far better than it was possible to imagine. But do not for a moment think that world difficulties are going to be over in a few months or a few years. For some years yet the turmoil will go on, and in some parts will get even worse. But eventually old controversies will settle down and the new world will gradually come in—the new era of spiritual development and understanding. Most of you who read this will live to see it transpire. The change will be far greater than you possibly could dream of.

The true idea of God is individualized in man. God wells in man. God expresses Himself in man, not merely in the prophets and seers of old, nor somewhere in the distant future, but in plain everyday people like us here and now. Once mankind has grasped this true concept of God, most of the evils of the present day will be swept into the discard, into obscurity, never to be seen again.

History, as we know it, is largely a chronicle of the faults and weaknesses of mankind, but that is because man has looked for God *outside* himself. Man has gone against the teaching of Jesus Christ and has tried to find God somewhere else than in his own heart. In this age of the second coming of the Christ, that is going to be changed.

To be perfectly clear about this we must ask ourselves, what is the Christ? The Christ is not Jesus. Jesus was the man who expressed the Christ more fully than anyone else. The Christ is the active Presence of God—the incarnation of God—in living men and women. This is the Christ and it is eternal. In the history of all races the Cosmic Christ has incarnated in man—Buddha, Moses, Elijah, and in many other leaders and teachers, but never to the degree the Christ manifested in Jesus. The reason is that Jesus, more than any other, had made himself aware of the Christ power. However, in this New Age, the Cosmic Christ will come into millions of men and women who are ready to receive It. This will be the second coming of the Christ for them.

In a very real sense, the Christ already lies dormant in the minds and hearts of men and women everywhere, waiting for that burst of recognition that we call the second coming of the Christ. In the meantime, every time we "salute" the Christ in another we are bringing that day closer in ourselves.

If you seek to experience the Christ other than by direct contact with God, you are doomed to disappointment. People have been forever attempting to take something less than God at firsthand. In the first chapter of Acts we find an extraordinary case of just this. Jesus selected twelve apostles. One of them was a failure and the other eleven persevered. After Jesus' transition they came together and selected another apostle to take the place of Judas, who had transgressed. Because they were not yet endued with power from on high but judged in human consciousness, they made a poor selection. They chose Matthias, a perfectly respectable person, but one who had not experienced the second coming of the Christ. The result? From that day to this no one has ever heard another word about Matthias. He looked the part and nothing more.

It is significant to note that the gap in the apostleship *was* filled. But the choice was not made by Peter, nor James, nor John, but by the Cosmic Christ Itself. It selected the last man whom the apostles would have dreamed of selecting—Saul, the persecutor. He became the twelfth apostle. And of course, when he got his illumination, his name was changed to Paul.

In a very real sense, there are two gospels, one hidden behind the other. There is the normal gospel with its face value, and there is the spiritual meaning of the Bible that is, so to speak, hidden behind the other. You may wonder why spiritual truth should be veiled in this way.

The answer is that the writers of the Bible wrote under divine inspiration, and they themselves did not always understand the full import of what they were saying or writing. That is not peculiar to the Bible writers alone. All of us do more than we realize when we speak or act. If we speak or act negatively we do more harm than we realize. And when we speak or act positively and constructively, we do more good than we know. And above all, our thoughts have more effect upon our own lives than we ever realize.

The Bible was written by men with a great deal of understanding, and very often the writer wrote to the highest he knew, but God put even more into it. Thus those who come centuries later—when the race has evolved more in consciousness—see things in it that the writers did not understand at the time.

This was true of Paul. He wrote a great many things, often in a complicated way, that have been misunderstood and misinterpreted. When Paul writes about Jesus coming with his angels, it means this Truth is coming into the world and into the hearts of the people. The general public is getting more and more of it. All the churches are teaching some of it—still using their own phraseology, of course. But the thing is there. Angels always represent direct inspiration, guidance, help. When one begins to realize the things that Jesus taught, how he gave all power to God and no power to outer conditions or negative circumstances, how he insisted upon always putting God first—this is Jesus coming with his angels into the individual's heart. If it were merely the popular conception of angels flying around, it might be startling, but it would not really mean anything.

It is the change in our hearts that counts. We need to remind ourselves constantly that nothing can do anything for us except a change within ourselves. For example, what does bad news do except to bring a change within ourselves? It generates fear, disappointment, frustration, etc. in ourselves. On the other hand, what does good news do except to bring a change within ourselves: joy replaces fear, happiness replaces misery, etc.? Nothing can act upon us except as it evokes something in us and through us. Thus, if Jesus simply came on earth and taught these things again and then went away again, what would such a literal second coming do for us? Very little except to remind us once more of what he said the first time.

However, when the Truth that he taught and the great spiritual power that he brought into the world come into our hearts, they change us completely. That is what the Bible means when it says, "The Lord Jesus shall be revealed from heaven with his mighty angels, in flaming fire." It means that this Christ Truth comes in a very vivid and real way into our hearts. It means a living realization of the Christ Truth.

The rest of the verse, when it is taken literally, sums up the fundamentalist teaching in many of the churches. It says, ". . . Taking vengeance on them that know not God, and that obey not the gospel of our Lord Jesus Christ: who shall be punished with everlasting destruction." This may make some people who believe they are saved, feel very comfortable. But does it sound like the Jesus who could forgive even those who crucified him? Could this come from Jesus who made forgiveness a cardinal point in the Great Prayer? Could Jesus, who made love of neighbor the test of whether or not you were a follower of his, have dealt in this spirit of vengeance?

The text was never meant to imply that Jesus would come back to punish people who knew not God. That is not the meaning. That is not the teaching of Jesus, and that is not the kind of God we worship. It means that when the knowledge and realization of the Christ Truth comes into people's hearts, it is not a cold and calculated thing. Rather, it comes like a flame of fire that transforms them and completely destroys fear. It destroys those things in ourselves that keep us back from God and it destroys them forever. It takes our limitations, our sins and sinfulness, our faults of character, and destroys them forever.

Those "that know not God" are not the people that do not go to a certain church, or people that we may not approve of. No. Those who know not God are the negative things in each one of us that are wiped out forever—when the Christ comes into our hearts. This is the second coming of the Christ for each one of us.

What does the second coming mean for the human race? Why are people talking about it so much today? It means that now is the time when the true idea of God is coming to all people. Narrow sectarianism is being dissolved and true ecumenism is coming to the fore. It is no coincidence that the space age and the second coming of Christ for the masses of mankind should arrive at the same time. The step forward always comes when man is ready for it. Moses and the early Egyptians could have had the automobile. Julius Caesar and the Romans could have had the telephone, but man had not yet made himself ready for those things. Always we have to make ourselves ready for the thing we want.

In all ages there have been outstanding souls who were far ahead of their time—and often were martyred or horribly persecuted for their beliefs. Yet Truth has a way of marching on. Columbus, for example, was one of those who was ahead of his time. Most of the leading lights of that day, including the clergy who were also the scholars, believed the world to be flat. In those days a man could lose his head for daring to teach the opposite, and some of them did. But Columbus stood firmly on his belief that the world was round and he was ready to prove it. And so another link in the chain of Truth was forged.

Man's expanding knowledge of the universe will also prove and disprove a great many other cherished theories and beliefs. He will be forced to drop his old narrow concepts of God—very often a God that has nothing else to do but watch the human race and mete out punishment for its sins. Expanding the horizons of space, man will discover that God is not only the God of the human race, but the God of the universe and of the many other races scattered throughout the cosmos. As the individual opens his heart to the Christ, he will understand more completely his relationship to God and the cosmos, and especially will he realize that this earth with its inhabitants is not an island unto itself.

Jesus, far-seeing seer, gave a hint. He said, "I have other folds that you know not of." And now we are on the threshold of knowing. Just as Jesus came in person two thousand years ago with a revolutionary new concept of man's relationship to God, the time is now here when there is beginning to be a real second coming in the hearts of men and women all over the globe. Jesus' teaching is being completely vindicated, understood, and accepted. The word "vengeance" in the Bible means vindication. Vindication of what? Vindication of the love and goodness and power of God. When you demonstrate the power of a human law, you are said to vindicate it. Demonstrating the power of God in your life is a vindication of spiritual law. God's truth and goodness are vindicated when the individual genuinely opens his heart to the second coming of the Christ.

CHAPTER 18

The Anatomy of Healing

*Thus saith the Lord God unto these bones; Behold, I will
cause breath to enter into you, and ye shall live.*

EZEKIEL 37:5

THE great thinkers of history have recognized
that man consists of body, soul, and spirit, and
that the key to controlling our lives lies in the
soul or mind—soul and mind being synonymous terms.
Plato, for example, remarked that we should never attempt to cure the body without curing the soul. Jesus went
much further and taught and demonstrated that it is the
mind that heals the body and outer conditions. Jesus
taught that whatever happens in the outer has had its inception in the pattern held in the mind of the individual. Everything originates in thought, and consequently,
if we hold sick thoughts, limiting thoughts, these are
going to be expressed in our bodies and in our circumstances.

Many of the Old Testament writers understood this
and the prophet Ezekiel is one of them. Ezekiel's story of

the Valley of Dry Bones is illustrative of this very idea, and gives a diagram, a ground plan, for any kind of healing. He puts his statements in the symbolical form so much used in the Bible, and he says, "They shall say, This land that was desolate is become like the garden of Eden; and the waste and desolate and ruined cities are become fenced, and are inhabited."

This is one of the many promises or statements of spiritual law in the Bible that says that those who think correctly and know the readiness of God to act, can turn any kind of disharmony into harmony and freedom. It tells us that if we know the Truth and cleave to it, the thing that is desolate shall become like the Garden of Eden, and the waste and desolate and ruined cities fortified and inhabited. Of course, this is a figurative way of speaking about our souls, for a city in the Bible always represents our consciousness.

Ezekiel is telling us that when we have trouble, sickness, fear, lack, when we are in sin, our souls are like a city that has been taken, conquered, and ruined. Usually when that has happened people lose hope. They become disappointed, depressed, and frustrated. They say, "What's the use? I haven't got a chance. Nothing seems to work. I'm finished. I'm ruined."

However, the Bible comes and says that there is no ruin except the belief in ruin. There is no evil and no limitation except the belief in evil and limitation. It says that if we insist upon seeing the Presence of God where disharmony seems to be, if we will insist on seeing God in that nagging, annoying situation, the waste cities, our consciousness, will be turned into the Garden of Eden—and that is a wonderful state of consciousness to be in.

In the Garden of Eden they did not have to fret about such things as rent or the latest fashions, and they had perfect social security. They did not have to worry about the thousands of things we worry about today. It was paradise. And here the Bible tells us that paradise can be restored—and, as usual, it tells us how. The answer is to recognize God as the only power. If we put God first, if we really say, "In the beginning, God," and mean it, and not put some idol—probably ourselves—in the place of God, then the power of God will come into our souls and bring healing and harmony and true success.

In chapters 36 and 37 of Ezekiel there are a number of references to Israel. As we have pointed out earlier, Israel means one who believes in God and in the power of prayer. To be an Israelite in the Bible sense, it is not enough just to believe in God. You must also believe in the power of prayer. If you say, "Certainly there is a God, but the laws of nature cannot change. Things are what they are"—you are not believing in the power of prayer. Unless you believe that prayer can change any condition in your life, or in someone else's, into harmony and success, you do not believe in prayer. You may believe in God, but the God you believe in is hardly worthy of your belief. If God is simply a formality and there is no way to change conditions through spiritual power, then what you have is determinism, materialism, and this is really the dethronement of God.

But this inspired writer tells you that you do have dominion. You have the power to take your life in your hands today and make it something worthwhile. Nothing that happened yesterday or ten years ago, or the fact that you failed to do something in the past, will prevent you from having harmony and freedom today. Other people may not understand this, but it matters not, because you have dominion over your own life. You can be free.

If there is some lack in your life—material, moral, mental—that lack can and will be abundantly supplied no matter what it is. It can, unless you prevent it by thinking, "This is too difficult . . . it is too late"—or something like that. This story in the Bible comes as a trumpet call to tell us that we must not accept less than perfect harmony and freedom and the joy that belongs to the children of God. The Bible says the children of God shout for joy. If you are not shouting for joy in your heart you are not expressing yourself as a child of God. You are claiming a different parentage altogether.

The first part of the story tells us about the glorious things that the knowledge of God brings: crops, herds, abundance of every sort. All the things that man can possibly want or need are his by his divine birthright as a child of God. And then the narrative goes on to the story of the Valley of Dry Bones.

Ezekiel, who wrote all this, was not merely trying to be poetical. He is one of the great prophets of the Bible. He was a man who had given much thought to God and man's relationship to Him. He was a man who learned practicality from the harshness of his times. He had seen his own country torn apart into two warring factions. He had seen sickness and misery and death on all sides. It seemed like a hopeless mess. Yet in his heart he knew that God had given him a message for humanity, not only for the Israelites of those days, but an ennobling inspiration for generations yet to come.

It was probably after one of the hundreds of battles that had taken place, when he had seen many slain in the field, that he began to ponder the questions: What could be done about it? What could God do about such a seemingly impossible situation? Was there any hope?

Ezekiel writes that he was taken away in the spirit of the Lord and set down in a valley that was full of dry bones. Valley in the Bible always means trouble and difficulty; while the hill or mountain is the uplifted consciousness. The great mystics and seers and teachers in the Bible are always spoken of as going up into the mountain to pray. This does not necessarily mean that the person actually went up on a mountain. The inference is that he got away from limiting thoughts and outer things to realize the presence of God.

So Ezekiel was taken away in the spirit of the Lord. In other words, Divine Inspiration came to him in a vision. In sharing that inspired vision, he outlined for all mankind a formula for spiritual healing. In the vision, the Lord said to him, "Son of man, can these bones live?" The son of man is your human personality, the thing you have so much trouble with. In other words, just how much faith have you got? And Ezekiel answered, "O Lord God, thou knowest." Ezekiel had enough faith to know that he could not do it, but God could.

This is the first step when you are weighed down with a difficulty and the thought comes to you, "Is there any way out?" The higher self says, "God knows. With God there is always a way."

And the Lord said, "Prophesy upon these bones." Pray over these bones. And Ezekiel calls out, "O ye dry bones, hear the word of the Lord. . . . Behold, I will cause breath to enter into you, and ye shall live."

This is a dynamic approach to the problem. It is the second step, the use of affirmation, spoken with authority. No shilly-shallying about it. No doubt. No hoping for the best. No thinking, "Well, if it doesn't do any good, it won't do any harm." Ezekiel was direct and to the point.

"Hear the word of the Lord"—the creative Word—"I will cause breath to enter into you, and ye shall live."

Every one of us could demonstrate over our challenges if we spoke with that kind of authority. And yet Ezekiel had nothing to go on but his faith in God. At first glance, what could be more discouraging than a valley filled with dry bones. Surely no problem could be more seemingly hopeless. But that is the very point. This great story of the Old Testament is a clarion call to the faithful, declaring that there is absolutely nothing that is impossible with God.

God says to the prophet and through him to us, "Speak the word and these skeletons will stand up. Pray for them and they will be covered with flesh. See My Presence in them and the breath of life will come into them, and they will be made living men and women." Ezekiel is really giving us the anatomy of a healing. He is telling us how to do it. It is the graphic description of the building of a wonderful demonstration.

Ezekiel knew what he was talking about. If he had not prayed often and demonstrated the Truth in his own life, if he had not been acquainted with grief, if he had not known what it was to weep, suffer, despair, and finally come through to the Presence of God, he would have turned these skeletons into living men in one quick jump. But his practical experience told him that this is not the way it works with human nature. We have to make our affirmations. We have to pray over the situation. We have to see the Presence of God where the difficulty seems to be. We have to overcome our doubts and fears. And only then does the action of God begin to become visible.

In the parable, first the skeletons stand up, but they are still skeletons. A foolish person might say, "Oh yes, I

got this small demonstration, but what good is that when
the thing I really want or need still seems to elude me. If
I have to have skeletons, they might just as well lie down
as far as I am concerned." Ezekiel sees the skeletons stand
up and then sinews and flesh and skin come upon them,
but still they are not alive. And the same doubting Thomas
will say, "What is the good of prayer. I am not getting any-
place. I knew this wouldn't work. They may have flesh
on them but still they are corpses. I don't want corpses
standing in my valley." They are still dead because they
lack the Spirit of God.

Ezekiel knew that the demonstration was not yet complete, but he also knew that what God begins, God fin-
ishes. He prayed some more. And he heard the voice of
God say to him, "Prophesy unto the wind, . . . and say to
the wind, Thus saith the Lord God; Come from the four
winds, O breath, and breathe upon these slain, that they
may live." Again we get a recognized Bible symbol. The
wind stands for the direct action of God, the Holy Spirit.
Jesus said, "The wind bloweth where it listeth," meaning
to say that the action of God takes place where the soul
is ready. Just as the apostles were breathed upon on the
day of Pentecost when "they were all with one accord in
one place." In other words, they were ready, and as a result they became new men who went out and changed
the world.

It is significant that in Greek, the word for wind is
"pneuma" and pneuma also means "spirit." It is the Spirit
of God that breathed on these skeletons, and the breath
came into them and they lived and stood on their feet,
an exceeding great army. This was the final step. The
demonstration was made. Ezekiel had realized that God
is Life, that in Him there is no death, that it is the Spirit

of God that quickeneth. The dry bones had stood up and become living men. That is symbolically the history of every demonstration.

Your life and mine, our body, our affairs, are the embodiment of our concept of God. As long as we have difficulty or limitation at any point in our lives, we have not grasped the truth of God at that point, and thus we embody the negative thing. What we understand we demonstrate, and when we understand sin, sickness, lack, and inharmony more than we understand God, we demonstrate those things—we embody them.

The action of God must be embodied. There is no cause without an effect and no effect without a cause. And so when the wind blew in that valley, the action of God was embodied as living people.

The prophets of old were an amazing group of men. They have no counterparts in modern society. We have had, of course, great leaders like Lincoln and Washington, and there is this much in common with the prophets of old: they all had incredible difficulties to meet, and each met them in their own way. What sets the prophets apart is that their main concern was to bring their people back to God. Other leaders have prayed to God for guidance, for mercy, for victory in a tight place. But the prophets always insisted upon putting God first and giving Him all power.

They knew the human heart because fundamentally they had to meet the same kind of difficulties that we have to meet. That is why this story of Ezekiel and the Valley of Dry Bones has a meaning for us in this day and age. Ezekiel knew that the Valley of Dry Bones was an apt description of his own soul, your soul, my soul, the soul of every man and woman regardless of when and where they might live. He knew that there are times when a person feels his soul is really a valley of dry bones, a valley of lost hopes and despair.

Unfortunately, there are many people whose consciousness is not much better than a graveyard of fears, doubts, worries, and frustrations. They have a choice collection of skeletons in the valley of their souls, enough to outfit several schools of anatomy for a long time to come.

But Ezekiel also knew that our souls can become the Garden of Eden, and he has given us the technique for restoring that desirable condition. There is no problem too big or of too long standing, no condition too powerful for God to change and make harmonious. Our hopes, our aspirations, our souls come alive as we take the dynamic approach that Ezekiel took.

CHAPTER 19

The Power in Your Name

And Moses said unto God, Behold, when I come unto the children of Israel, and shall say unto them, The God of your fathers hath sent me unto you; and they shall say to me, What is his name? what shall I say unto them? And God said unto Moses, I AM THAT I AM: and he said, Thus shalt thou say unto the children of Israel, I AM hath sent me unto you.

EXODUS 3:13–14

THE origin and meaning of names is a fascinating study in itself, but nowhere are names more significant than in the Bible. They not only designate important people, places, and things, but because they have symbolical meanings as well, they become for you and me important diagrams for living. That is why Moses was so insistent upon knowing the true name of God.

Shakespeare poses the eternal question, "What's in a name?" He had a deep insight into metaphysics and much of his writing is veiled in symbol and allegory. The characters in his plays, the greater *and* lesser characters, are dramatizations of certain aspects of the human soul. Every page of Shakespeare contains occult truths for those who can perceive them. The answer to his question, "What's in a name?" can be found, for instance, in his Romeo and Juliet. The boy symbolizes the spirit and the girl the soul or psyche. It was because they did not understand this fundamental relationship that their lives came to grief. And it is because we do not understand the relationship of spirit and soul that our lives are filled with problems and difficulties.

One of the great names of the Bible is Abraham. Abraham was a real person who lived thousands of years ago; but the story of his life comes in the early part of the Bible because his life is used as a living parable. Abraham stands for rational faith, and rational faith is the beginning of the spiritual life. The Bible starts out with a general history of the human race, but the first person of real consequence from the psychological and spiritual point of view is Abraham, or as he started out in life, Abram. Abram did not learn of his real or spiritual name until he had demonstrated the willingness through faith to follow the light of God wherever it led.

Abram was a Chaldean living in that part of the world. It was a nation of idolators, but in that respect they were not very much different from a good many people today. They worshiped palpable idols of wood and stone and metal. Our idols are more subtle. We call them money, position, power, and pull, and we rationalize this by saying, "Oh yes, I believe in God, but in business and my daily affairs, I have to take a commonsense point of view."

However, Abram was not satisfied with this approach to things. Tradition says that he was very wealthy. He was a patriarch and had position. From the material point of view he should have been satisfied, but he was not—

because in his heart he wanted something that these things could not provide: a living contact with God. Under the guidance of God he left all this and launched out to find a new life in a strange land. This did not mean that Abram had solved all his problems for all time, but it did mean that in times of need he turned to God first for help and guidance. The text says that "God tempted him." Now we know that God, Divine Love, never tempts anyone. What happened was that the unfolding of Abram's nature presented difficulties that he had to overcome. And through his faith and his overcoming, both he and his wife had their names changed.

In the beginning he was Abram and his wife was Sarai. And then something very unusual and important happened. A letter was added to their names. Not just any old letter like K, L, P, or B—but an H. H is the aspirate, the letter where you breathe, and breath stands for inspiration. The Bible speaks of the breath of God, and you will remember that Jesus breathed on his apostles and said to them, "Receive ye the Holy Ghost." So Abram was changed to Abraham and Sarai to Sarah. Of course this is all symbolical. Just arbitrarily putting an H in your name will not mean much. There must be a basic change in your soul, and then you become aware of your secret name.

This happened to Paul, too. Before he had his revelation on the road to Damascus he was Saul. But with his awakening to the Truth of Being, his name was changed to Paul. In the case of Abraham, he received a promise because of his faith that "in thee shall all the families of the earth be blessed." In other words, through Abraham's experience and the Bible that came to be written, all the nations of the earth will learn in time the power of faith in God and in prayer.

Every person has a secret name known to God, and when you get your inspiration, your illumination, you will receive a new name. Revelation says, "To him that overcometh will I give . . . a white stone, and in the stone a new name written, which no man knoweth save he that receiveth it."

Now, we may ask ourselves, "What *is* a name?" A name is the sound of an idea. If I say "rose," you think of color, fragrance, and the shape of a rose. Or you think of a time you gave roses to your best girl, or that one rose that reminds you of him. If I should say "lily," "carnation," or "skunk cabbage," an entirely different set of pictures comes into your mind. So the name of a thing is the sound of an idea or ideas. The name of a person, place, or thing sums up the nature or character of that thing. The name of God ought to sum up the nature or character of God, and so it does.

Up until the time of Moses, the people did not know the sacred name of God. All through Hebrew history the name of God was considered very sacred, the mysterious secret known only to the initiated. This secrecy concerning names is seen in the primitive races too. Primitive peoples are much closer to the race mind, and there are many things we are learning from their customs. One of their customs was to keep the name of a child secret until the proper time and then there was a great ceremony. This was true among the American Indians. They usually gave names to their children that they thought summed up the character or qualities, like Running Deer or Laughing Water. The early gypsies did this too. They kept the name of a child secret because they instinctively felt that the name was the key to his real character or nature.

Moses reflected this general secrecy concerning names and about the Great Name in particular when he asked, "When I come unto the children of Israel, and shall say unto them, The God of your fathers hath sent me unto you; and they shall say to me, What is his name? what shall I say unto them? And God said unto Moses, I AM THAT I AM.

It is a statement that has puzzled religious people down through the ages. In this tremendous statement we find the complete name of God. God is unconditioned being, incorporeal, without beginning or end, the eternal, ever-ready, ever-present help. Jesus further develops the idea when he says, "God is a Spirit: and they that worship him must worship him in spirit and in truth."

I AM THAT I AM is the complete and final name of God. Any other statement would limit Him in some way. So we begin to see that to know that name gives man power because it identifies the true nature of God. The more we understand the true nature of God the more we will understand our own natures and the power we possess. For make no mistake, there is power in your name when you know how to use it. You may say, "Well, I've been around a few years and my name hasn't carried too much weight. Oh, names like Rockefeller, Du Pont, and Rothschild may wield power, but not mine." That may be quite true on the surface, but we shall see that there is great power in your *true* name.

The priesthoods of the ancient world, and some of the modern ones too, have tried to keep the masses in darkness about the nature and character of God. It has been their aim to make people lean on an organization, while knowledge of the nature of God might make them too independent. Thus the name of God was kept secret because they have felt that spiritual power was summed up in the name of God.

Throughout the Bible the writers speak of the Name of God or the Name of the Lord. For instance, when the Queen of Sheba, whom Jesus called the Queen of the South, came to visit Solomon, the Bible says that she came to test him with hard questions. She came to inquire, not about God, or about the Lord, but about the NAME of the Lord—thus again emphasizing the Name.

The key to the name of the Lord is found in what we call Jehovah, the personalized God of the Old Testament. Here we begin to get a sense of God expressing Himself as Man. Pure, unconditioned Being—I AM THAT I AM— has now become differentiated as men and women. The word Jehovah is an anglicized version of the Hebrew, which was made up of four letters, Yod, Hé, Wau, Hé— spelling "Yevé." These four Hebrew letters represent the masculine and feminine principles, and in this form they mean one God expressing Himself in the souls of men and women. The Hebrews went further with this idea of God and added suffixes, Jehovah becoming Jehovah-ramah, Jehovah-jire, and so on—God as peace, God as health, God as abundance, etc.

God incarnates as Man in you and me, and because we are expressions of God, we share His power; but we have to know this. So it is not surprising that the ancient priesthoods of the Egyptians, the Babylonians, and the Hebrews kept the name of God secret in order to consolidate their own power over the masses. But people have intuitively felt that there was a Word of Power that would give dominion. In many of the secret orders, some of which have come down to the present day, there is a search for the "lost word," the lost secret that would give the key to life. Man has been given the hope that if he will wait a little longer, or strive a little harder, he will be given the secret. The years have passed. He has waited, and worked, and gained some other insights. But the secret of the Lost Word of Power has eluded him.

In the 30th chapter of Deuteronomy, verses 12 to 14, Moses reveals the secret, and hundreds of years later Jesus identifies himself with this lost Word of Power. It is strange that we could have missed it. Moses clearly says, "It is not in heaven, that thou shouldest say, Who shall go up for us to heaven, and bring it unto us, that we may hear it, and do it? Neither is it beyond the sea, that thou shouldest say, Who shall go over the sea for us, and bring it unto us, that we may hear it, and do it? But the word is very nigh unto thee, in thy mouth, and in thy heart, that thou mayest do it."

What is the lost word, the secret Name of God in you? *I AM.* This is the great secret of the so-called lost word. This is the philosopher's stone of the alchemists, and it is really the secret lying behind all religions and all philosophies.

I AM is your true identity. I AM is your real name, and in that name there is power. I AM is Divine Spirit, your real eternal self. It was never born and will never die. I AM is never sad, never grows old, never worries or sins or knows fear. However, this I AM is filtered through your consciousness and so you have the power of misusing it, as many people do. You have free will and the power to choose whether you will use it constructively or destructively. You can attach the I AM to your true nature and experience great power, or you can misuse it by misrepresenting yourself in many limited ways.

When you say, "I am," the natural question is, "I am what?" It has to be qualified, and when you qualify it, you limit it. If you say, "I am a man," that means you are not a woman. "I am an American" means you are not a Frenchman or a Spaniard. When you complete the I AM, you limit the expression in one way or another. But God is unlimited, I AM THAT I AM, unexpressed, creative power, Divine Mind waiting for expression. God has to be expressed, and Man is God in expression. I AM THAT I AM becomes I AM. Therefore Moses is told, "Thus shalt thou say unto the children of Israel, I AM hath sent me unto you."

Man is one with God, the self-livingness of God, and thus he has the power to attach the I AM to all the attributes of God: freedom, joy, health, success, abundance. Always I AM connects you with Divine Power because you are the I AM of the I AM THAT I AM. I AM is the Word of Power. It is the presence of God in you. It insures that you can go direct to God, that you do not need any intermediary.

All through history, back to the days of Babylon and Egypt, people have been led to believe that they needed an intermediary to approach God, and the Pharisees and the priesthood of Jesus' time tried to do the same thing. However, Moses was instructed to tell the people that God dwells among His people, that the Word of Power is in their mouths and hearts—I AM. That does not mean that someone else cannot pray for you or give you spiritual help. It means that you can and should go to God direct. Every time you say, "I am," you are using the power of God to bring certain things into your life, and what you bring will depend upon how you use the I AM and what you attach to it.

The name Jehovah was given to the people thousands of years ago and later written down in the Bible, in order that people might know they are one with God, to know that God is the ever-present help waiting to redeem and save. It is the knowledge that the love of God shines through and says, "I am your God and you are my people. I AM THAT I AM but you are I AM, my beloved son in whom I am well pleased."

Jesus knew the power of the I AM and he used it in many constructive ways. "I am the good shepherd . . . I am the door . . . I am the bread of life. I am the way, the truth, and the life." These expressions were commonplace in his everyday teaching. But there were occasions when he gave special significance to the I AM, emphasizing its mystical quality.

Chapter 8 of the Book of John—and John reports the highest teaching of Jesus—gives a good deal of insight concerning the cosmic nature of the I AM. Jesus was teaching in the temple, in the part called the treasury, and he began to speak to the crowd, saying, "I am the light of the world. He that followeth me [my teaching] shall not walk in darkness, but shall have the light of life." The Pharisees immediately took exception, claiming he was bearing false testimony of himself. Jesus patiently explained that he was not speaking of his own mind but as he was inspired by the Father. But they would have none of it. As Jesus himself said, there are none so blind as those who will not see.

Finally, to press home the point that he was not referring to Jesus the man but to the Cosmic Christ, he said to them, "If ye believe not that I am *he*, ye shall die in your sins." Here we have one of those words in the Bible that are printed in italics. This occurs whenever a word was missing in the original manuscript, and the translators put it in italics to show that the word was supplied by them. However, in this case the word "he" was not in the original. The translators erroneously inserted it, thinking it was necessary grammatically to complete the sentence.

But Jesus is not speaking about himself. He is saying that unless a person believes in the I AM, the Indwelling Christ in every man, he has misunderstood his relationship to God, and he will die without knowledge of the Word of Power.

Jesus continues this thought by saying, "When ye have lifted up the Son of man, then shall ye know that I am *he*, and I do nothing of myself; but as my Father hath taught me [inspired me], I speak these things." Again the italicized word was erroneously inserted. The meaning here is that when we come to a true understanding of man's relationship to God, then we shall know that I AM is the presence of God in each one, and that that presence gives dominion.

Then Jesus said, "Ye shall know the truth, and the truth shall make you free." This statement covers many facets of man's life, but in this context it has a special meaning. The Bible says that there were those in the crowd who answered, "We be Abraham's seed, and were never in bondage to any man: how sayest thou, Ye shall be made free?" Jesus told them they were judging after the flesh but if they would change their minds and understand that the Son—the I AM—has all power, then they would be free indeed and no longer have to rely upon intermediaries, or upon some supposed good that came out of the past. And he added, "If ye were Abraham's children, ye would do the works of Abraham," for Abraham was a man of great faith who always put God first. Again they accused Jesus of being a liar. He replied, "I seek not mine own glory. . . . Verily, verily, I say unto you, If a man keep my saying, he shall never see death. Then said the Jews unto him, Now we know that thou hast a devil. Abraham is dead, and the prophets; and thou sayest, If a man keep my saying, he shall never taste of death. Art thou greater than our father Abraham, which is dead? and the prophets are dead: whom makest thou thyself?" Intentionally or otherwise they were completely misunderstanding the tremendous import of what Jesus was teaching.

Said Jesus, "Your father Abraham rejoiced to see my day: and he saw it, and was glad. Then said the Jews unto him, thou art not yet fifty years old, and hast thou seen Abraham?" Jesus ended his dissertation, saying, "Verily, verily, I say unto you, Before Abraham was, I am." Jesus was giving emphasis to the mystical nature of the I AM. It is the Cosmic Christ that has always existed but that came to its fullest expression in the person of Jesus. I AM is the eternal self that was never born and will never die.

On another occasion, when Jesus came into Caesarea Philippi, he questioned his disciples, "Who do men say that I the Son of man am?" In other words, "Who do the people think I am?" And his disciples replied, "Some say that thou art John the Baptist; some, Elias; and others, Jeremias, or one of the prophets." In passing, it should be noted that the people of that day had a strong belief in reincarnation, for they were in fact saying that Jesus was a reincarnation of one of the prophets.

And then Jesus turned the question to the disciples themselves. "But whom say *ye* that I am?" And Simon Peter answered and said, "Thou art the Christ, the Son of the living God." And Jesus answered, "Blessed art thou, Simon Barjona: for flesh and blood hath not revealed it unto thee, but my Father which is in heaven."

Jesus could say, and did, "I am the Christ," and so can you. Each one has a secret name known to God, and when you get your inspiration, your illumination, you will receive a new name. In Revelation we read, "To him that overcometh will I give . . . a white stone, and in the stone a new name written, which no man knoweth saving he that receiveth it."

If you merely think of yourself as Tom Brown or Mary Jones with your aches and pains and bills to pay, you are not thinking with power. But if you say, "I am Tom Brown, the Christ," or "I am Mary Jones, the Christ," then you are identifying yourself with the Eternal and the good. Now, make no mistake, you are not saying you are Jesus, the Christ. You are simply voicing your true identity as a child of God, Tom Brown or Mary Jones, the Christ. This is your new name, which only you can use. It is fulfilling the prophecy that Jesus made, "The works that I do shall [ye] also do. . . . Is it not written in your law, I said, Ye are gods?" Thus Jesus becomes the great diagram for living, and I AM is the Way by which we can follow him in a personal demonstration of the Christ.

Perhaps it may sound a little strange to you at first to say that you are Tom Brown or Mary Jones, the Christ; but then, every new thing seems strange at first. Later you will say to yourself, Why did I not recognize that long ago?

When there is a problem that seems difficult to solve, think to yourself, "I am so-and-so, the Christ." Then think what that means. Can the Christ be sick? Can the Christ be in lack? Can the Christ be stymied by any problem? Of course, if you are going to refer to yourself as Tom Brown or Mary Jones, the Christ, it will be necessary for you to give more than lip service. Your actions must also be in accord with that high ideal.

There is power in your true name when you know how to use it. I AM THAT I AM is the Great Name, and I AM is the greatest name short of that.

CHAPTER 20

The Resurrection of the World

*For as yet they knew not the scripture, that he must rise
again from the dead.*

JOHN 20:9

T HE people who lived and worked with Jesus
Christ, who knew him intimately, who listened
to his teaching and heard his promises—for
the most part these people never realized the full import
of his mission, that he must die and literally rise again
from the dead, a complete and perfect man. They did
not fully understand that, and all through the ages right
down to the present time, Christian people as a whole
have not understood it either.

Indeed, there are those who go so far as to say that the
Crucifixion may have happened, but they cannot believe
the Resurrection as historical fact. "It is a beautiful story,"
they say, "but obviously a myth." They ask for some sort
of proof that either of these things actually took place.

There should be nothing hard to understand about
the Crucifixion. It was a fairly common occurrence in

that day. Just as we have had capital punishment by means of the electric chair or by hanging, the Romans had crucifixion. It was strictly a Roman punishment and not Jewish. The Jews sometimes stoned malefactors to death, as they wanted to do with the woman taken in adultery. So when Jesus was convicted under Roman rule, crucifixion was the normal punishment.

The Resurrection, however, is a different story. It needs corroboration to be believed. For hundreds of thousands of years before Jesus appeared on earth no one had ever resurrected his body, and I might add that no one has done it since. There was that handful of people before Jesus who had translated their bodies, but they did not make a reappearance on earth.

What proofs are there that the Resurrection did indeed take place? There are a number of them. After the Resurrection, Jesus appeared to two of the disciples on the road to Emmaus. He appeared a number of times to the apostles, sometimes in closed rooms, sometimes in the open. He was able to satisfy a doubting Thomas that he was not seeing a ghost, but a real live, flesh-and-blood person. On another occasion he built a fire on the shores of the sea of Tiberias and had breakfast waiting for some very tired apostles who had been out fishing all night. At one time he appeared to a group of five hundred people. And even Paul bases his apostleship on having seen the risen Christ on the road to Damascus. Paul was so convinced of this that, having persecuted the early Christians with might and main, he made a complete about-face, and became one of the greatest exponents of the teaching of Jesus and his resurrection.

However, I believe there is even greater proof than this of the Resurrection. All of the apostles, with the exception of John, died violent deaths, Peter himself being crucified upside down in Rome. All of these men had gone out around the Mediterranean basin, giving the teachings of Jesus, preaching his resurrection, and healing the sick and the maimed in his name. In those early days, belief in the Resurrection and second coming of the Christ was the test of the true believer. If the Resurrection had not happened, do you think these men would have gone out risking their lives, being beheaded or crucified, for a myth? No, they had been eyewitnesses of the Resurrection, and they were ready to stake their lives on it.

The Resurrection did take place, but the mass of the Christian people for these two thousand years have not grasped the real significance of it. Thus they have celebrated the feast of Easter faithfully, but with limited understanding, largely missing the true import of what Jesus came to teach and to do. However, now, in this New Age that we have entered, the time has come when all the people are going to understand this wonderful mystery. Knowing the Truth and practicing it, the human race will at last take the same step that Jesus took and share in his triumph.

Easter is the festival of triumph. It follows what is traditionally called Holy Week. The word "holy," in the context of our metaphysical study, means whole and complete, not sanctimonious. It means physical health; it means freedom of the soul, peace of mind, and that unity of life that is the will of God for men and women. Easter signifies nothing less than this. For many people Easter commemorates a marvelous event that happened nineteen centuries ago. But they feel it has little bearing on the present day, and thus the Bible, in one of its great moments, loses its spiritual import. Easter is not a thing of the past, but a grand and glorious awakening for us today and tomorrow and for all the days to come.

Long before Jesus came on earth, long before Abraham went out into the new land, the festival of Easter was observed. In the ancient civilizations, long before written history, people kept the festival of springtime, because that is what Easter is. Man has always celebrated the coming of spring with special rites and ceremonies, for he has intuitively felt that regeneration and resurrection are part of the law of life. The true law of our lives has no part in death. Death is not part of God's scheme. By the fundamental law of nature, all living things constantly renew, fulfill a cycle, and renew. The seasons have followed one another, never failing through all the millions of years that the solar system has been in existence. Following winter, spring has always come. The trees seem to die away. The leaves fall off, the flowers decay, but spring comes and they are renewed. Men and women have felt that this process had a special message for them. So always there has been the spring festival following the vernal equinox.

Then Jesus came to the earth. He taught, worked, suffered, and finally died that we might realize that we can make Easter a real thing for ourselves. Jesus, of course, need not have died had he not wanted to. He could have dematerialized his body and gone away to the presence of God without dying, as others had done. But he wanted to make it possible for us to follow him in the regeneration and resurrection. Sooner or later, as individuals, and as a race, we have to overcome death. Death is the last enemy that shall be overcome. When we have overcome death then we shall have accomplished Easter, and our work will be done. That will be the end of fear, the end of sickness and decay, the end of sin and limitation.

A time is coming when the human race is going to overcome these things. There are those who say that man is necessarily sinful and can never be otherwise. Such an idea is spiritual blindness and an insult to God. Sin, sickness, and limitation are not part of God's plan for us. Sooner or later we are going to overcome them. All the things that make life on earth so difficult—sickness, fear, threats of war, aggression of one nation against another, one set of people in terror of another set of people—these things will all disappear. Do not listen to the pessimist, for he is at heart an atheist. The truth is that God is good, and as the human race realizes this more and more, these things will disappear.

For hundreds of millions of years the seasons have told us this story again and again. The winter of doubt and fear and frustration will ultimately disappear for the whole human race. Spring will come with its promise, and summer with its fulfillment. That is the story of Easter.

In the life of Jesus Christ we know that Calvary preceded Easter. Jesus had to go through great suffering on the cross—not physical suffering. The driving of nails through his hands, and pressing the crown of thorns upon his head in the hall of Pilate, did not physically hurt because with his knowledge of Truth, he was easily able to demonstrate over pain. Terrifying as physical pain may be, the worst physical suffering is not nearly so bad as mental suffering. On the cross Jesus had to tune in with all the fear, hatred, resentment, remorse, lust, and terror in the race mind, past, present, and future, and rise above it. And that he did.

Calvary had to precede Easter because that is the story of the human heart. No one who has ever done anything really worthwhile in spiritual development has been able to get there without paying the price. There is no such thing for any of us as getting into the kingdom of heaven without paying a price. Never does Easter morning dawn without the Friday of Calvary preceding it.

The Gospels of Jesus do not say that salvation is a cheap thing or that resurrection is easy. They do not say, "Just take an optimistic outlook; hope for the best; be as happy as you can; and all will be well." That kind of cheap optimism has no place in the Bible teaching. The Bible says that because we are men and women and have free will and self-determination, we are certain to have limitations and difficulties to overcome. Of course, knowledge of the Truth leads us to the realization that all the difficulties that we have to meet are within us. Anything that seems to attack us from the outside is really but the projection of something within. We have these things in us and we have to overcome them. The overcoming of them involves Calvary. The cross must be overcome first. It is a symbol far older than Christianity. In the ancient world it stood for limitation. So the cross must be overcome. The true symbol of Easter is the circle, which is the symbol of eternity, of spiritual things. The circle, or solar disk if you like, represents triumph.

The great tragedy of Christianity is that so often the churches and the clergy have taught Calvary, leaving the symbol of the cross and its suffering as the last word of the Christian message. Now, it is right that people should have been taught the story of Calvary and what it means. But to send people out into the world with the idea of the cross as the last word is to hobble them psychologically, to impoverish them spiritually. It has left people discouraged and depressed; with their faith and understanding of God undermined and weakened, for it bolsters the erroneous theological concept of the Fall of Man. This is not what Jesus Christ wanted, and certainly it is not what he taught. The last word in the Christian message is the risen, triumphant Christ—perfect man, perfect soul, perfect union with God. So let us let go of the Crucifixion, cross out the cross of Calvary, and go on to the Resurrection.

Jesus Christ rose again because he had overcome the belief in separation from God. What theology calls the Fall of Man is the belief that we are separate from God. The Truth is that we are not separate—we are the expressions of God. It is as though God is singing a song and that song is man. We are the very self-livingness of God, not created in some past time, but re-created every moment. Because God lives, we live, for we are part of God's self-expression of Himself. Yet people have the belief that they are separate from God, and the Cosmic Law is that what we really believe we experience.

It is this basic feeling of being separate from God that fills man with fear, and under the domination of fear, he does strange things. He begins to choose the lower instead of the higher. He believes he can get some supposed gain by lying or cheating or stealing. He believes he is "on his own" and must fight his way in the jungle of human experience. This belief in separation from God is the major tragedy of human existence, giving rise to many negative things that are faults of belief and not of fact. As soon as we begin to realize our oneness with God, everything changes and everything regenerates.

Jesus was born of a woman, inherited all the race beliefs, and then had to spend his early years in understanding them and mastering them. He had to grow "in wisdom and stature, and in favor with God and man." Finally, he completely overcame the sense of separation from God in what we call the Resurrection. His body was dematerialized by his thought. Once that is done, the body can always be reproduced again by thought, and that is what Jesus did.

It was early in the morning on that first Easter Day. It was quiet in the garden where Jesus had been laid. The crowds had long since gone. Jesus had been taken down from the cross and his body wrapped in grave clothes as was the custom. The people had murmured one to another, "Who would have thought this could happen? He was the most popular man in Jerusalem. Why, only this past week some had called him Christ, the King; and others had shouted Hosannah to the Son of David. Who would have thought it could all happen so quickly, this sudden turn of events?"

So Jesus was buried in a new tomb and the entrance was sealed with a large stone. It was all over. The crowds went their way, people shaking their heads in resignation and muttering, "Well, dead is dead." Not all the people. Not Mary Magdalene. She had loved Jesus so much that she was the last one at the crucifixion, and now she was the first at the sepulcher. She came while it was yet dark, just before daybreak, that magic moment when there was a mist rising from the fields and the veil between the two worlds is a little thinner than at other times.

Most of the Hosannah-shouting followers of Jesus had gone away after the triumphal march into Jerusalem, and forgot. It is so easy to jump on the bandwagon and beat the drums while the parade is passing by; but let the hubbub cease and these same people disappear as if into thin air. Even some of Jesus' apostles were in hiding for fear of the authorities, and certainly a number of his disciples thought that in the end Jesus was a failure, for—as the Bible so pointedly says—they understood not that he must die and rise again from the dead.

The world does not admire failure even if it is a glorious failure. The world admires success, and nothing succeeds like success with most people, even if it is not the worthiest kind of success. Sometimes in our finest moments we may seem to be a failure, at least to those who look with mortal eye. We may even seem a failure in our own self-image. This is the very time that we need to remind ourselves of the Resurrection story, for it is not the story of defeat but of victory.

Yes, Mary was there at the tomb. She had not forgotten. In her heart of hearts her woman's intuition had told her that in some way she would see him again. Love always finds a way. She was there at the sepulçher . . . and to her surprise and perhaps dismay, she found the stone rolled away from the entrance. Peter and John were off a little way and she rushed over to them, exclaiming, "They have taken away the Lord out of the sepulchre, and we know not where they have laid him." Her first thought was that the Roman soldiers had come and taken the body. Peter and John ran to the tomb. Peter was an older and more stocky man, so John outran him. In a moment Peter caught up to him. And Peter—nothing shy about Peter— went into the tomb first with John behind him. They found Jesus gone . . . but curiously the grave clothes with which he had been bound were lying on the floor. If the Roman soldiers had taken the body away they would not have taken time to unwrap the body and leave the grave clothes behind.

Peter and John were perplexed because they too at that time did not really comprehend that Jesus must literally rise again from the dead. So they went their way to tell the others. But Mary stood there weeping, in a half-expectant hope that her love for Jesus would somehow lead her to find him. And then, not knowing why, she stooped down to look into the sepulcher and saw two angels in gleaming white.

As we have said in a previous chapter, there are those who say, "It is an interesting story, but there are really no such things as angels, and therefore Mary couldn't really have seen them." And there is logic in what they say as far as their own perception is concerned. Such people will never see angels until there is a spiritual change in themselves, because those who see angels are those who believe in angels.

Unless you believe that the whole universe is the living garment of God, and unless you believe that His angels are everywhere, you will never see angels. If you believe in angels then angels will come into your life. They will not be the conventional figures that the artists portray, but they will be messengers of God. As Paul says, "Some have entertained angels unawares." God sends angels whenever you are ready for them and need them. Angels are God's inspiration. They are the courage God sends in time of difficulty. They are the material aid God provides in an emergency. They are the increase in understanding that is needed to get your healing or your demonstration. The more we believe in angels, the more certain it is they will be on hand when we need them.

Mary saw the angels and they had a message for her: "Why seek ye the living among the dead?" With that she turned away, not completely comprehending the message. She had not yet gotten her awakening to the true state of affairs. She still thought of the dead Jesus instead of the living Christ. That is what so many people do when some loved one has passed on. They cling to that which they knew and loved, which is understandable. But in the light of what Jesus taught and demonstrated, should we not look to the risen Christ of that loved one? This is perhaps one of the hardest lessons any of us will have to learn. Death is not extinction but a divine promotion.

Well, Mary needed another reminder before she was fully awakened to the Truth. As she turned away from the tomb, in that dim early morning light she saw a man whom she believed to be the gardener. He asked, "Woman, why weepest thou?" Mary, still laboring under a false belief in death, replied, "Tell me where thou hast laid him, and I will take him away." Jesus uttered just one word, "Mary." That was enough. There was instant recognition of that beloved voice she had so longed to hear again. Now it all came back to her. She remembered what he had promised, that on the third day he would rise from the dead. Yes, she had forgotten the Truth, even as we do. We have to be reminded again and again and again of it. We turn to other things first, and we find ourselves seeking a living demonstration among the dead cares and hopes of yesterday.

In sudden recognition of Jesus, Mary cried out with joyous exultation, "Master." She had found him, and as you might expect a woman to do, she ran over to kiss him. But Jesus said to her, "Touch me not; for I am not yet ascended to my Father." This was the first time that he had materialized his body and the demonstration was not quite complete. When we make a demonstration we are not to touch it, so to speak, until we are absolutely sure of it. So many people dissipate their spiritual power by telling everyone about the marvelous demonstration they have made, only to find that it has evaporated into thin air. Later on, when Jesus had reproduced his body a number of times, he invited Thomas and the others to touch him and see that it was really he with flesh and bones like everyone else. By then he was absolutely sure of the resurrection demonstration.

But here at his first appearance he said something to Mary that is very significant for each one of us. He said, "Go to my brethren [my disciples] and say unto them, I ascend unto my Father, and your Father; and to my God, and your God." This gives Easter its true significance for us. It is a magnificent diagram for living as sons of God, for Jesus was claiming for us ultimately everything that he claimed for himself. Not God on one side and man on the other. Not Jesus the divine and man the human. "Say unto them, I ascend unto my Father, and *your* Father." Jesus is designating us as brothers with a common parenthood. In other words, there is no difference between us and Jesus except in degree. We are not different from him in kind.

This is our charter to spiritual freedom. Jesus is declaring that there is no limit to what any individual can do and become if he understands the Resurrection story, for the Resurrection is the culmination and vindication of the whole of Jesus' life and teaching. In other words, Jesus regained his unity with God, and that regaining of unity meant complete dominion over the body and circumstances.

All evil is a belief in separation from God. Not actual separation, for there can be no real separation, but a *belief* in separation. If the Resurrection means anything at all, it must mean that sooner or later we have to do the same thing—and that is exactly what it does mean. We have to make the same demonstration that Jesus made, if not here and at this time, then somewhere else at another time. Jesus did not do the work for the whole human race once and for all. He was the way-shower. We have free will and self-determination. We suffer only for our own mistakes—not for somebody else's. The work of Jesus on Calvary and at the Resurrection made it possible for us to do it for ourselves, and each one must do it for himself.

Now, we do not have to die to demonstrate the power of resurrection. I say we do not *have to*, if we can completely overcome the belief in separation from God. Please note that I am not saying we shall not die. What I

am saying is that if any one of us can overcome the sense
of separation from God—and that means also overcoming the sense of separation from our fellowman—then
we shall not die. We shall be translated. Moses did not
die; Enoch did not; Elijah did not; John the Divine, the
writer of this account of the Resurrection, did not. They
overcame that sense of separation. But may I repeat, we
must also overcome that sense of separation from our
fellowman. As long as I can see danger in another human
being, as long as I condemn or resent another human
being, I have not begun my unity with God. "He that
loveth not his brother whom he hath seen," says John,
"how can he love God whom he hath not seen?"

It is the message of love again, so often stressed by
Jesus and the others. If we want to follow Jesus in the
great demonstration, we must cleanse our heart of hatred, jealousy, fear, resentment, and condemnation, and
fill our heart with a true divine love for all human beings everywhere no matter who they may be. To realize
divine love for all without condemnation or hard feeling of any kind is the road we all must follow if we want
to make the eventual resurrection demonstration.

In the course of human experience progress for man
sometimes seems impossibly difficult, but this is because
we are in the thought of limitation, dependent upon material things, and thus subject to "the law of the flesh."
However, when we catch the vision of the Cosmic Christ
and identify ourselves with that, we no longer come under
the law of outer things, but, as Paul said, under grace.
No human being ever lived who was more under bondage
of law than Paul. He was so steeped in it from his earliest
days that he almost lost his faith in God. Then he realized
the Truth one day, and hundreds of years later, Luther,
reading those wonderful words that Paul wrote, was also

set free in the same way: "The just shall live by faith."
This means that when you see the vision of the divine
possibility within you and stretch forth your hands toward it, you are no longer under the law of sin and
bondage. The limitations and weaknesses of your own
character, the mistakes of the past, no longer have the
slightest power to keep you back. You are under the law
of grace.

Calvary is past and Easter morning is dawning. It is the
dawn of Easter and never again will you have the Thurs-
day or Friday to go through. You are under grace. This is
the real law of scientific prayer. It is withdrawing yourself from the limited condition into the spiritual realm
where there is freedom and dominion.

How do you withdraw yourself? By some physical act?
No. It is a matter of attention. When your attention is
centered on limitation, on your weaknesses or other people's weaknesses, on your difficulties, your sickness, your
fears, you are in bondage to these things. As Paul says,
"His servants ye are to whom you obey." But when you
lift your attention—your I AM—out of the limited things
into the spiritual, then you are in a state of consciousness where the limiting things no longer have any power.

This is why scientific prayer performs miracles right
and left. This is why it turns people's lives upside down,
takes them out of beds of pain and sickness, and brings
them out of lives of sin and self-contempt. Scientific
prayer does this—not now and again, not occasionally,
but every day in the week in every quarter of the world.
It does it whenever and wherever one raises his consciousness to the presence of God.

Easter is the crowning diagram of our personal destiny. Easter is there to impress upon us, to drive home
to us, to brand into our hearts, that the resurrection is an

activity that God calls for in all humanity, not just in Jesus. Jesus showed the way. The resurrection is a practical step for you and me to take today. It is not just a theological belief. It is a fact of nature. It is the Truth of Being. It means a perfect body. It means peace of mind. It means a perfect and integrated soul. It means reunion with God in thought, understanding, and realization. It means the overcoming of every limitation. We can do it; we have to do it; and in the name of Jesus Christ, we shall do it.